MAGNIFICENT ITALIAN VILLAS AND PALACES

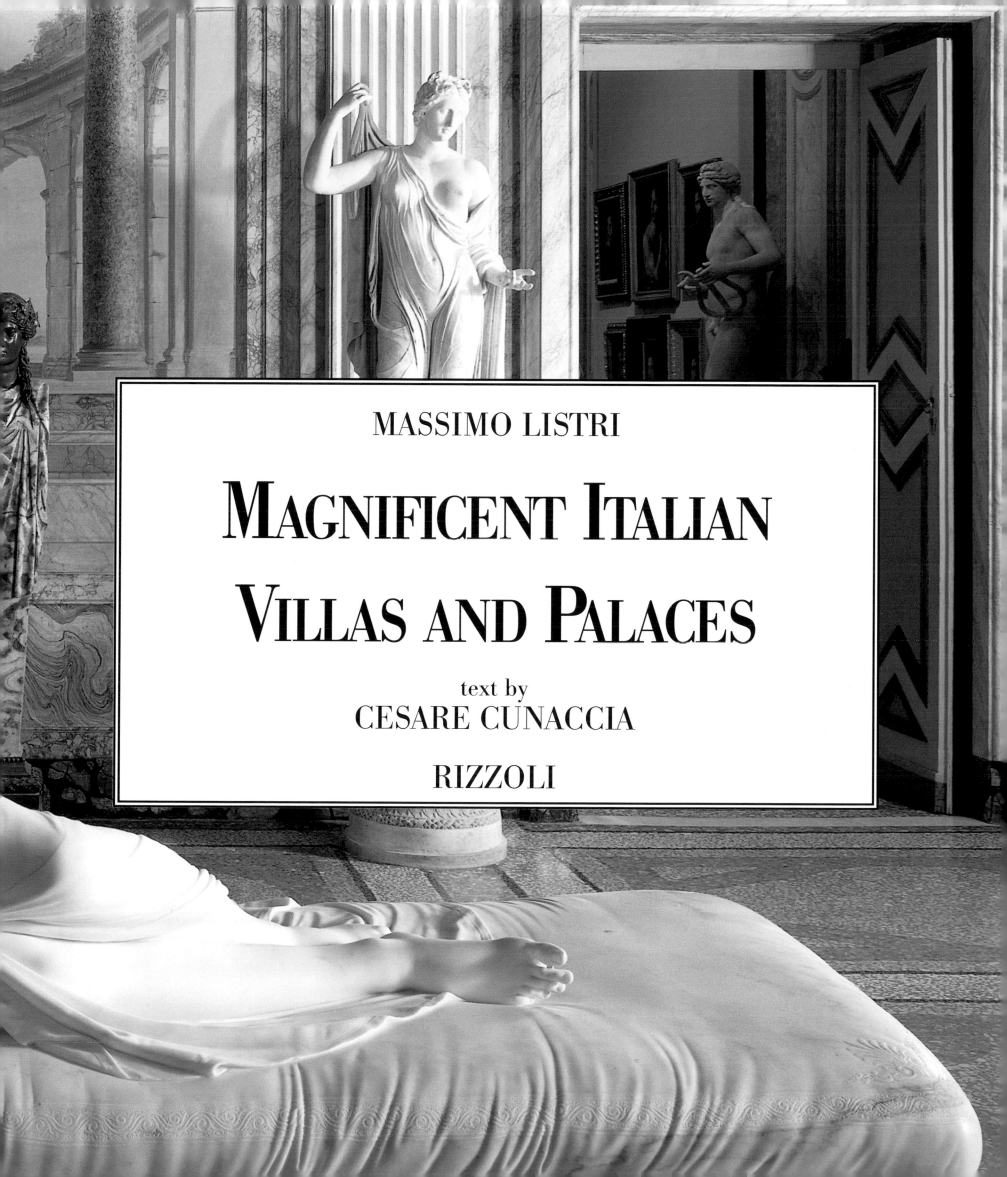

MASSIMO LISTRI

MAGNIFICENT ITALIAN VILLAS AND PALACES

text by
CESARE CUNACCIA

RIZZOLI

First published in the United States of America in 2004 by
Rizzoli International Publications, Inc.
300 Park Avenue South
New York, NY 10010
www.rizzoliusa.com

© 2003 MAGNUS EDIZIONI SpA, UDINE, ITALY
Translation by Giles Watson

2004 2005 2006 2007/ 10 9 8 7 6 5 4 3 2 1

Printed in Italy

ISBN 0-8478-2591-4

Library of Congress Control Number: 2003107955

Contents

PREFACE

"The past does not exist," Alberto Moravia used to mutter obsessively to his friend Cesare Garboli when they visited Fondi and the Monti Aurunci. Moravia had spent many difficult months in the area during the Second World War, and was able to

point out here a plant, and there a dwelling, a couple of bushes or a spring. "The past does not exist." We shall never know whether the past is real or imaginary. The past is a province in a fairy tale, suspended in the midst of pain, beauty, and freedom. It is a universe of mirrors and an infinitely arbitrary, yet exciting, itinerary of metamorphosis. Anyone who wants to engage with the thrilling, illusory weave of memory must make the effort to trace the filigree of that supramundane sphere from the start. Its dark choices must be accepted, its denials and revelations digested. An attempt must be made to belong simultaneously to two adjacent, complementary macrocosms.

Below left: Lake Como seen from one of the many windows at Villa Fontanelle.The villa was purchased in 1977 by Gianni Versace and became one of his best-loved homes.

Below right: A bathroom at Villa Fontanelle, beautifully decorated in the neoclassical style.

The journey we embarked on took us to some of Italy's most glorious residences, and note that these are only some of the thousands of superb homes that have been built over the centuries up and down the peninsula. We took it as

Facing: An entrancing view of the loggia at the Medici villa at Artimino in Tuscany. Its main feature is a scenic three-flight staircase, constructed in 1930 by the architect Enrico Lusini.

axiomatic that these edifices were neither remains from, nor documents of, a time that is irremediably gone and now distant, codified, deep-frozen in the dogmas of history. For that reason, the path we chose took us into the misty, timeless perspective of narrative and analysis. It breaks down the consolidated barriers that imprison memory and sever the silken thread that binds past events, everyday chronicles, and the signs left by art in a closed, defined environment as cold and invulnerable as a diamond. This approach puts the emphasis on re-evocation and the narration of events that are often extremely well-known. It involves abandoning the self to those events while holding on to what is solid and real in the powdery mist of dreams. The *palazzi* and villas tell us an infinite number of stories teeming with unforgettable figures, private lives, and astonishingly extravagant ceremonies. They are caskets that contain the will for power, for solemn magnificence, and of a deep-seated aesthetic belonging. These residences could only be Italian in their ever-different, ever-changing, stubbornly special appearance. They evince a vocation that is a marvelous combination of monumental theatricality, illusion, pathos, poetic suffusion, and exquisitely private spaces.

Everywhere, we perceive the irresistible, indispensable, life-bringing influence of art. It is art to be enjoyed in the secrecy of a *studiolo,* a *Wunderkammer,* or a Chamber of Curiosities. It is art that proclaims the political and intellectual manifesto of a noble house or, as in the case of the Gonzagas at Mantua, became synonymous with the family itself, the actual and symbolic representation of the *gens.*There are city-shaped *palazzi* and gigantic houses built on the scale of the owner's boundless ambition; stages for pomp, circumstance, head-turning pride, and on occasion bitter delusion. The mazes of halls and rooms are here melancholy and there vibrant, spectacular remains from a time apparently lost, and from habits and cultures that continue despite the traumatic interruptions of time. In every case, the villas and *palazzi* tell us of the people who built them, lived in them, or guided their expansion and transfor-mation from one generation to the next.

14

"Italy is a country that is always afraid of losing what it never had," Roberto Calasso claimed in *I Quarantanove Gradini* (The Forty Nine Steps).

In these residences, we will not only see famous treasure troves, art collections of stunning splendor, imposing or transfigured architectural creations, Edenic or Leibnizian gardens, and sumptuous furnishings, but also secret, perhaps unappreciated, homes looked after with passionate love and dedication. We will also see materializing across the centuries images from myth and legend, musical cadences, sibylline allegories, dazzling promises, lineages of visionaries or practical achievers, and mysterious understatement. In a treatise on the art of laying out gardens, an eighteenth-century British gentleman claimed that the Italian approach was superior for the beauty and harmony of its proportions, aristocratically hidden behind the modesty of its enclosures. His thesis was that expectations were deliberately kept just below reality to engender the additional thrill of wonderment. The Italian garden harbors a revelation, a coup de théâtre. The motto of Lorenzo the Magnificent, one of the emblematic figures on the tapestry we have tried to weave, was *Le Temps Revien* (Time Returns). It is time without Kronos, *Zeit ohne Kronos*. Let us rip aside the dark cloak of chronology and boldly follow the circular, redeeming path of Proustian time.

Palazzo Cattaneo Adorno

Genova, Liguria

"I began to make occasional visits to the proud city many years ago . . . the magnificent sea air, the fathomless skies in the paintings, the savor of the food and the haughty reserve of the people bewitched me. Above all else, I loved—and still do love—the sense of splendor that seems to underpin the tone and taste of the ancient *palazzi*. Architecture dictated the rules to the inhabitants. 'A marble facade,' said Montesquieu, 'but inside only a serving woman, spinning.' True, the Genoese are thrifty, but the buildings are unforgettable. Facades and furnishings—gold glitters all around and the azure of lapis lazuli abounds, distributed generously for once." This passage from *L'Armadio delle Meraviglie (The Cabinet of Curiosities),* by Alvar Gonzalez-Palacios, captures perfectly Genoa's innermost aesthetic essence, its reserved, secret, aristocratic soul, and the subtle, captiously contradictory emotions the city can arouse. Unique and inimitable, Genoa can be a cold, cutting Naples, or another Lubeck, a Hanseatic city transplanted to the Mediterranean. The intricate maze of the city's *carruggi*, or narrow lanes, and its spacious piazzas, are liberally sprinkled with opulent ancient residences, some with surprisingly extensive and significant privately owned art collections. The *chiaroscuro* of pomp-bedecked seventeenth-century Genoa had its focal point in Via Balbi, built between 1602 and 1620, and commissioned by the noble Balbi family from the Como-born architect, Bartolomeo Bianco.

great Bernardo Strozzi and the tenebrist Giovanni Battista Langetti. Then the third generation in the early eighteenth century brought the light-filled art of Paolo Gerolamo Piola and Lorenzo de Ferrari. Outside contributions came from Titian, Veronese, Camillo Procaccini, Simon Vouet, Guercino, Reni, Domenichino, Caravaggio, as well as the Gentileschis: father and daughter, who left for England from Genoa.

During his stay in Genoa, the sophisticated Flemish gentleman-painter Anthony van Dyck was a guest in a wing of the new *palazzo* built by Bartolomeo Bianco for the noble Gio Agostino Balbi, who died in 1620. The Ticino architect

promised "to maintain upstanding and free of fissures the Palazzo and apartments for one year and one day, and to construct it sound, using good materials, and wood, and ironmongery." The date was 7 February 1618. It was here that van Dyck painted portraits of Gio Agostino Balbi's entire family. The seventeenth century would see more new civil and religious buildings rise along the Balbis' august new thoroughfare. Outstanding among them were Palazzo Reale, Palazzo Balbi Cattaneo, restructured by Stefano Balbi between 1614 and 1649, and the Jesuit College. The college, now the main building of the university of Genoa, was

The lengthy sojourn of the greatest of Peter Paul Rubens' disciples, Anthony van Dyck, who stayed in Genoa from 1621 to 1627, roughly coincides with the heyday of the indigenous aristocracy. Trade, and myriad links with the Holy Roman Empire and northern Europe, brought unimaginable wealth to the city. The now prosperous local aristocrats built up an aura of legend by having themselves portrayed beruffed and severe in black, in lavish fashionable costume, or laden with pearls against the backdrop of spectacular gardens or purple drapes swollen by baroque-inspired breezes.

Political and commercial decline would inevitably overtake the city in the latter half of the eighteenth century. Genoa lost its colonies in the east and the king of Spain began to struggle to meet the obligations he had contracted with the city's bankers. In the early seventeenth century, however, competition was fierce among the nobility of "Genoa the Superb" to flaunt wealth as spectacularly as possible. Residencies were lavishly furnished with tapestries, silverware, curiosities, and valuable furnishings. Art collections included works by leading local painters, such as Luca Cambiaso, Bernardo Castello, Lazzaro Tavarone, and Domenico Fiasella. After Rubens and van Dyck had left their mark, these artists were joined by contributions from the

Santi Gerolamo e Saverio, now the university library, erected for Francesco Maria Balbi in 1650. The residence of Gio Agostino Balbi today known as Palazzo Durazzo Pallavicini, belongs now to the noble Cattaneo Adorno family, which continues to exercise its stewardship with profound love and dedication. The heritage, intact and continuously enriched over the centuries, comprises furniture, especially beautifully proportioned and embellished locally made eighteenth-century items incorporating the latest comforts and novelties of the day from France, as well as row upon row of ancient oriental ceramics and items from major European porcelain and pottery manufacturers. There are sumptuous fabrics and ornaments, baroque sculptures by Filippo Parodi, a vast historical archive, and a huge collection of paintings hanging on the walls, along with marble, jet-black Lavagna stone, oriental rugs, brocades and *potiches*, frescoes, mirrors, and bronze or gilt flaming torches. The residence exudes a sense of magnificent, centuries-old civilization. Memories are coaxed back to life with diligent care and attention, conjuring up a Proustian sense of times past, the circular suspension of linear chronology, and the healing of the wounds that separate past from present.

built by Bartolomeo Bianco between 1634 and 1639, and further embellished with the spectacular monumental staircase by Domenico Parodi in 1718.

Then there is Palazzo Balbi Senarega, which has also become a university building. Its large and very significant collection of seventeenth-century frescoes is the work of Valerio Castello, Gregorio de Ferrari, and Domenico Piola. Further examples are the church of Santi Vittore e Carlo, Palazzo Raggio (formerly Palazzo Francesco Maria Balbi built in 1618) and the church of

Above:
The great staircase presents a spectacular neoclassical-style "domino" structure, designed by the architect Emanuele Andrea Tagliafichi between 1774 and 1780 for Marcello Durazzo II.

Right:
An ornate gilt wood kneeler graces the small private chapel. In the foreground is a seventeenth-century marble bust of Gianluca Durazzo by Filippo Parodi.

Facing:
The gilt pilaster strips of the *Salotto di Bacigalupo* terminate in elegant Ionic capitals. The vaulted ceiling is dominated by an imposing eighteenth-century crystal chandelier. Elegant Imari vases stand on the shelves.

Molding his creation to the slopes of the Pietraminuta hill, Bartolomeo Bianco isolated the building from the surrounding townscape, gracing it with four wings and two lateral gardens. The huge, austere Via Balbi facade exploits to the full the limited street frontage available. Simply designed windows, with no projecting architrave or hood mold, trace an abstract pattern of filled and empty spaces along the compact, unyielding mass of the wall. This leaves the main door, the imposing cornice, and the loggias on either side the task of lending agility and movement to the facade.

The Durazzos, a recently ennobled Genoese family of Albanian origin, entered the building's history in the person of Giacomo Filippo II (1672–1764). Throughout his long life, Giacomo Filippo II constantly ordered new work on the architectural fabric or interior decoration. He also acquired many superb works of art for the collection he dreamed of putting together, challenging Genoa's great patrician families in this field, as in others. Giacomo Filippo II's dreams were realized, perhaps to a greater extent than he himself hoped, and the present-day collection is formed by the amalgamation of the two main picture galleries. In 1871, the Durazzo collection from Via Balbi was enlarged with the paintings that Ignazio Pallavicini kept in the *palazzo* named after him in Via XXV Aprile to form a single, astonishingly complete and distinguished whole. Some of the rooms that surround the central courtyard are named after the artists whose works they house, as is the magnificent entrance hall, which is adorned with the works commissioned by Marcello Durazzo II between 1774 and 1780 from Andrea Emanuele Tagliafichi. The painter Paolo Gerolamo Piola and the *quadraturista*, or perspective artist, Francesco Maria Costa, who contributed to the restoration of the works, also assisted their patron in selecting and arranging his treasures. Around 1723, the pair labored together, frescoing the vaults of the two rooms looking onto Via Balbi on the right and left of the vast *Salone di Achille*. These two rooms bear illustrious names. One is dedicated to Anthony van Dyck, whose extraordinary portraits of the Balbi family rivaled the mastery of Domenichino and Ribera, while the other is named after

Guido Reni. In the meantime, more artists were hired. Bologna-born Tomaso Aldovrandini and Giacomo Antonio Boni, and Andrea Procaccini from Rome, all worked on the *Sala del Bacigalupo*, the *Sala della Maddalena*, and the *Sala di Muzio Scevola* rooms, as well as the *Salotto Giallo* and *Salotto Verde*, while Giacomo Antonio Boni and Giacomo Giuseppe Davolio were called in for the vault of the vast *Salone d'Achille* in 1735. This lavish makeover in the seventeenth and eighteenth-centuries still characterizes the opulent decorative scheme of the interiors at Palazzo Durazzo Pallavicini.

The embellishment and expansion of this noble residence were destined not to end in the third decade of the eighteenth century. Giacomo Filippo III, who died in 1812, was a man of wide-ranging cultural interests who established a library and a museum of natural history. From 1774 to 1780, Marcello II made alterations to the access areas of the building, asking Andrea Emanuele

Below and facing:
Two of the rooms that house this marvelous collection. It was formed in 1871 when the Durazzo family's paintings from their Via Balbi residence were joined by the works Ignazio Pallavicini brought from his own *palazzo* in Via XXV Aprile.

Facing and below:
These two views of the gallery show some of the many ornaments and precious *objets d'art* to be found at Palazzo Cattaneo Adorno. The superb sedan chair, with its gilt *chinoiserie* decoration, is indicative of the fascination that the Far East held for Europe's aristocracy in the eighteenth century.

Tagliafichi to restructure the previous entrance hall, depicted by Jean-Honoré Fragonard in a sketch from 1761. Tagliafichi lowered the internal courtyard by more than five feet to create the dramatic structure of the neoclassical great staircase we see today. The configuration introduces the solemn lines of the *piano nobile*, where Tagliafichi created a gallery marked off by Ionic columns, concluding the renovation work in the neoclassical idiom. Giuseppe Berlendis assures us in his *Raccolta delle Migliori Fabbriche ed Ornamenti della Città di Genova* (Anthology of the Finest Buildings and Ornaments in the City of Genoa), published in Milan in 1828, that Tagliafichi had made a notable contribution to the cityscape just prior to the republic's sad, final destruction at the hands of Napoleon, "exciting awe and admiration in all its contemporaries."

PALAZZO BALBI-DURAZZO

GENOVA, LIGURIA

The seventeenth century dawned under the most favorable auspices for Genoa's oligarchy. For nearly five decades, the Genoese had been leading players on the international financial scene. Between 1552 and 1556, they had acquired fifty-one percent of the debts contracted by the emperor, Charles V. Since then, as the historian Fernand Braudel asserts, "Genoa discreetly dominated Europe," extending credit to Philip II and Philip III, and thus becoming a crucial mainstay in the construction of the Spanish imperial system.

For Genoa, it was a *Siglo de Oro*, a golden century illuminated by unprecedented economic and artistic splendor. Legends grew up around the great warriors, such as Andrea Doria, known as *Il Principe* (The Prince), Admiral Giovanni Andrea Doria and Ambrogio Spinola, commander of Spain's armies in the Low Countries and Italy from 1604 to 1631. Commerce thrived, ostentation was rife, and the city's appearance was transformed. Artists flocked to Genoa from far and near. The new, emerging patricians needed a distinctive imagery of their own so they consigned themselves to myth in the semblances proposed by the portraits of Sofonisba Anguissola and Artemisia Gentileschi, or were transported to Olympus by the radiant, heroic, *magniloquence* of Rubens and van Dyck. Between 1550 and 1558, those same families marked out the area of Strada Nuova. They were followed, in the early seventeenth century from 1602 to 1620, by the Balbis, inspired by family pride to lay out, entirely on their own initiative, a broad avenue flanked by magnificent *palazzi*, joining Piazza dell'Annunziata to Porta San Tomaso. This was the Strada dei Signori Balbi.

More of a theatrical set than an urban thoroughfare, the Strada dei Signori Balbi was designed by the Como-born architect Bartolomeo Bianco and inspected, in the early seventeenth century, by an admiring Pieter Paul Rubens. In 1622, Rubens would bear witness to its splendor in a superb series of engravings that drew the attention of the whole of Europe to Genoa's grandeur, its noble residences, its marble staircases, and its spectacular gardens.

The historical events that accompanied the building of Palazzo Balbi-Durazzo, now known as Palazzo Reale, are very similar to those surrounding the nearby Palazzo Durazzo-

Facing:
The sumptuous *Galleria degli Specchi* was decorated by cele-brated Genoese artists like Domenico and Filippo Parodi, and Francesco Maria Schiaffino, as well as by the Carrara-born Francesco Baratta.

Left:
View of the *Galleria degli Specchi* from the adjacent room. The family's influence is apparent in the furnishings and rocaille décor. Note the graceful colored stuccoes over the door.

Below:
This neoclassical sculpture in the *Galleria degli Specchi* is a bust of Giovanni Battista Balbi with an angel. Giovanni Battista was the son of Stefano, the original owner of Palazzo Reale.

Pallavicini. Both were erected for the Balbis, and both later passed to the Durazzos, another family that had only recently come into prominence and was steadily gaining influence in business circles, at least until financial crisis struck Genoa in the third decade of the seventeenth century. The building's name was later changed to Palazzo Reale, when it was purchased for the house of Savoy, in 1824, by Carlo Felice. When the *Strada Nobilium De Balbis* had been laid out, and the residences of the various family members built, Stefano Balbi drew up the contract for the construction of his new home with architects Pier Francesco Cantone and Michele Moncino. Stefano was a key figure in the ambitious ramifications of the Balbis' economic and political power. He was active in the silk trade and had close business contacts with Flanders, where a branch of the family had moved, becoming important traders in the Antwerp market. Stefano died in 1660, having in 1607 married Clelia, the daughter of Silvestro Invrea, doge of Genoa.

The original building was somewhat less imposing than the *palazzo* we see today. It comprised simply a robust, square construction, the architecture of whose facades conformed to the sixteenth-century model established in Genoa by Galeazzo Alessi. The long facade, which extends for almost 328 feet, had yet to be built. Palazzo Balbi entered a golden age when it was acquired by Eugenio Durazzo, who belonged to an extremely wealthy family of Albanian origin that had recently been elevated to the Genoese nobility. Durazzo inherited the property in 1677 and, mindful of the dazzling magnificence of noble residences in Rome at the time, immediately embarked on a rebuilding program to transform his new home into a majestic, baroque complex. The two wings were added, then Durazzo extended the main prospect from Vico Pace to Vico Sant'Antonio. Subsequently, in 1679, he acquired the adjacent Teatro del Falcone, which was thus incorporated into the immense new construction. The central upper story dates from the same period.

Eugenio Durazzo's architectural ambitions and appetite for image enhancement appear to have been boundless. In 1705, his increasing desire to Romanize the residence prompted him to summon from the Eternal City the great architect Carlo Fontana, whose classicist style, which fused the French sense of proportion with the monumentality of Roman baroque, was gaining favor across

Above:
This neoclassical console resting on gilt sphinxes is emblematic of the sumptuous atmosphere of the *Sala delle Udienze*.

Facing:
Detail of the ceiling in the duke of Genoa's bedroom. The spectacular stuccoes and frescoed decoration open onto an illusionistic perspective thronging with gods and allegorical figures.

Below:
The rooms on the *piano nobile* are in a continuous sequence along the main facade. This was a genuine innovation for residential building in seventeenth and eighteenth-century Genoa.

31

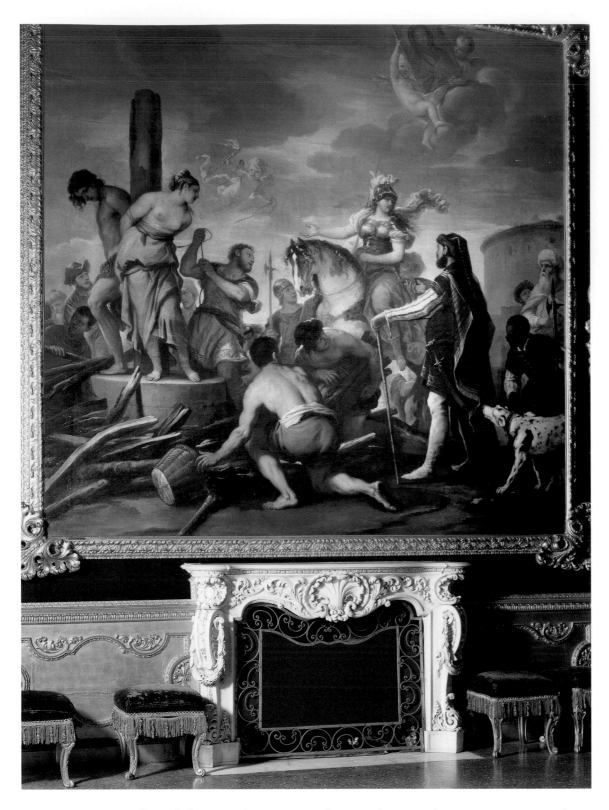

elegance, already hinting at rocaille, pervades the room. It is achieved by unexpected illusionistic effects that bring into play stuccoes, frescoes, mirrors, ancient and baroque sculptures, as well as the stunningly graceful Genoese chandeliers. Naturally, the artistic, didactic, and moralistic impact focuses on the exaltation of the house of Durazzo, whose coat of arms is proudly displayed in the central span of the ceiling. Decorations *en grisaille* cover the walls, separated by mirrored pilasters that are themselves adorned with vegetal motifs, picked up by the footstools. Delicate gilding enhances the capitals and ornamental moldings, framing the colorful frescoed narrative in the vault. The *Galleria degli Specchi* demonstrates how far stucco technique had evolved in Genoa. The tradition in the genre began at the height of the sixteenth century with the complicated mannerist repertoire of Perin Del Vaga, a disciple of Raphael in his years in Rome, for Andrea Doria's residence, the Palazzo del Principe. It continued at Tobia Pallavicino's *palazzo* in Strada Nuova, and in the Villa Pallavicino delle Peschiere by Giovanni Battista Castello, known as *Il Bergamasco*.

The overall concept of the gallery is certainly Domenico Parodi's, but a large group of artists, decorators, and painters contributed, including the great Filippo Parodi, who created the sculpture of *Venus and Hyacinth* at the entrance, Francesco Maria Schiaffino, and the Carrara artist, Francesco Baratta, from whom were commissioned the statues of two celebrated queens of antiquity, Cleopatra and Artemisia. Other interesting features are the ducal antechamber, which boasts a splendid ceiling fresco by Valerio Castello, and the chapel gallery, where the walls were decorated by two leading exponents of the baroque style in Europe, Giovanni Battista Carlone and Giovanni Andrea Carlone, who executed the decorations above the doors.

Palazzo Reale still hosts an impressive collection of paintings, including works by Anthony van Dyck, Domenico Tintoretto, the Bassano family, Giovanni Battista Castiglione, called *Il Grechetto*, Pittoni, the Genoese artists, Domenico Fiasella and Valerio Castello, whose plundered *Rape of Proserpine* was returned here from Palazzo Madama in Rome, and Luca Giordano's *Olindo and Sophronia*, dating from 1680. This superb sequence evokes the splendid collections of the Balbi and Durazzo families, although the Palazzo Reale's greatest artistic treasure was the great

Europe. Fontana aligned the portal, entrance-hall and staircases perpendicular to the facade, imposing a completely new rhythm on the edifice, especially the side facing the sea.

Exquisitely Baroque, and equally surprising, is the contrast between the solemn, austere Via Balbi frontage and the color-led, Bibiena-style theatricality of the seaward-facing facade. The coup de théâtre that redefines the *palazzo's* entire spatial and stylistic harmony is the *corte d'onore*, or main courtyard. It is not square, as was the custom in the sixteenth century, but instead was laid out as an

elongated rectangle to create a second courtyard, marked off by the elevated screen of the double arcade that frames the vast terrace overlooking the harbor. The layout of the interior features a long succession of rooms on the *piano nobile*, or main second story, traversing the entire principal facade. The astonishing scenic impact of the *Galleria degli Specchi*, or Gallery of Mirrors, adorned with lavish white and gold stuccoes, was contrived by Domenico Parodi. Completed about 1730, it follows the model of other similar seventeenth- and eighteenth-century galleries in Rome. A subtly poised

Facing:
This imposing canvas of *Olindo Saving Sophronia from the Stake*, which hangs in the throne room, was painted about 1680 by Luca Giordano. It is only one of the many works that are still held in the collection at Palazzo Reale.

Right:
A fine oil on canvas portrait of Caterina Balbi Durazzo, painted in 1624 by Anton van Dyck, conserved in the gallery at Palazzo Reale. The social standing of Caterina, the first owner of the *palazzo*, is clear from her lavish attire, her three-string pearl necklace, and the diadem in her hair.

Feast in the House of Simon the Pharisee, by Paolo Veronese. The work lent its name to the rococo room, where it hung until 1837. Since then, it has been replaced by an excellent seventeenth-century copy by David Corte, commissioned by Giovanni Filippo Spinola, who owned Palazzo Reale immediately before the Durazzos. Carlo Alberto of Savoy, to avoid provoking the indignant reaction of the citizenry, removed the canvas to the newly established Galleria Sabauda in Turin. The removal of Veronese's canvas was the first act in a systematic despoliation and neglect that has only recently come to an end.

loans. Frescoes, sculptures, and the hundred-odd paintings in the collection emerged from under a blanket of dust and oblivion, as did furniture, hangings, doors, decorative floors, windows, fireplaces, and wall lights as restorers strove to recreate the harmonious unity of the objects that had made the building a major European noble residence. The restoration campaign aimed to evoke the same "lived-in" atmosphere described by Lady Morgan for 1919 after a visit to this noble *palazzo*.

When the entire building was restored a few years ago, work was based on a scientific study of the *palazzo's* historic inventories. Simultaneously, a campaign was launched to request the return of works and individual objects that had left the residence on temporary

Above:
A neoclassical console table in the *Sala delle Udienza* bearing the initials of Carlo Alberto under a Savoy crown.

Facing:
The king's bedchamber is adorned with two valuable paintings. The *Crucifixion* by Anton van Dyck hangs across from an *Allegory of Summer*, attributed to Bartolomeo Guidobono.

Castello di Guarene
Cuneo, Piedmont

The imposing bulk of the castle at Guarene was erected by the Roero family on high ground with good visibility. For centuries, it was a symbol of the feudal prestige of one of Piedmont's leading noble houses. Rising high over a majestic, sweeping panorama that embraces Monferrato from Monte Rosa to the Maritime Alps and the celebrated vineyards of the Langhe, the great eighteenth-century residence we see today is merely the most recent incarnation of a fortress that was erected here in the twelfth century, when hostilities broke out between the towns of Alba and Asti. Since time immemorial, the hill has been crucially important as a strategic location from which to control the surrounding territory. In the fourteenth century, Guarene was an outpost of the marquisate of Monferrato under the Paleologo family, who made their capital at Saluzzo a lively hub of Renaissance culture. For three centuries, the castle suffered the consequences of its privileged position. Life at Guarene was frequently disrupted by sieges, marauding armies, and battles large and small. Then in 1707, Monferrato passed from the Gonzagas of Mantua to the Savoys, putting an end to hundreds of years of intrigue, warfare, diplomatic coups, and secret negotiations.

In the late seventeenth century, the Roeros of Vezza and Guarene chose the site as their permanent residence. At that time, Guarene was not so much a splendid noble residence as a large, but uncomfortable and obsolete, fortress left over from a dark and distant past. It was then that Count Carlo Giacinto Roero of Guarene came on the scene. A patron of artists and musicians and a distinguished

Facing:
The main facade of Castello di Guarene overlooks the Italian garden, whose attractions include an arrangement of ornamental hedges, lemon trees, and rose bushes. The garden was laid out by Count Carlo Giacinto Roero.

early eighteenth-century expert on fortifications, Carlo Giacinto completed a huge program of extension and restoration at the family *palazzo* in Turin, capital of the kingdom of Sardinia. From 1725 until 1736, he turned his attention to Guarene.

In that decade, Carlo Giacinto decided to demolish the crumbling walls of the old fortress to erect a new and much more magnificent building. He took charge of the project personally, drafting detailed architectural plans and even designing ornaments and furniture for the interior of his superb new home. He was active at a crucial time for the Savoy kingdom, which lay in an important strategic location, wedged between the great European powers. The kingdom had been unified and enlarged, thanks to the shrewd foreign policy tenaciously pursued by the Savoy rulers. In the early eighteenth century, after the War of the Spanish Succession, it experienced a wave of extraordinary historic transformations and a splendid flowering of the arts. Carlo Giacinto Roero, refined gentleman and amateur builder, was a pupil of the great Messina architect, Filippo Juvarra. As artistic consultant to King Vittorio Amedeo II of Savoy, the warrior monarch who

Facing:
Over the great staircase is a plaque commemorating the visit in 1773 of Vittorio Amedeo III, duke of Savoy.

Below and above:
The castle has a well-stocked library. Above, a marble bust.

earned Piedmont a prestigious place on the European political scene, Juvarra was, with Carlo di Castellamonte, the leading figure in the splendid eighteenth-century revival of Piedmontese building, especially for the royal house, after the baroque fireworks of Guarino Guarini in the previous century.

The residence's first stone was laid in the afternoon of September 13, 1726. A few years later, the essential features had been built and the formal garden was laid out. In 1778, the elliptical, domed family chapel of Santa Teresa was built. The castle's massive bulk is brought to life by screen effects at the four corners, its imposing spaces proudly reminiscent of its ancient feudal and defensive roles. It is still a far cry from the airy, exquisitely rocaille configuration created by Juvarra a Stupinigi. Set on a high base, with jutting cornices, and lent interest by its theatrically alternating floors, Guarene dominates the surrounding landscape. On the south side, it looks onto a lovely Italian garden laid out in 1740, where the formal geometry of the topiary conjures up attractive perspective effects. Inside, the rooms are sumptuous and exquisite. In Piedmont, a land that has drunk deeply at the spring of French influence, the eighteenth century also witnessed an extraordinary revival in the applied arts. It was home to the greatest Italian cabinetmaker of the day, Pietro Piffetti, who made whimsically sophisticated rocaille furniture of dizzying virtuosity, with masterful ivory and mother-of-pearl inlay and scenic rhythms heightened by asymmetry, color, and contrasting materials. Guarene boasts the remarkable *Stanze Cinesi*, or Chinese Rooms, whose India Company tapestries were purchased in London, again in the eighteenth century. The taste for chinoiserie was a particularly popular decorative fashion that reached exceptional heights in the rococo of Piedmont. It culminated in another piece of Juvarra genius, the *Gabinetto Cinese* in Palazzo Reale at Turin, sixty boards for which were purchased in 1732 at Rome, "or pieces of wood with black and gold lacquer, flowers, and animals of China." That is to say that imported Chinese lacquered panels and porcelain were purchased, for the room, and skilled craft workers hired, including the celebrated Pietro Massa, an expert in Chinese lacquerware. The sharp-tongued, witty Président de Brosses, visiting Turin in 1740, remarked at Palazzo Reale, where Piffetti had profused the best of his art, the *Gabinetto Cinese*, "*cela est magnifiquement triste*" (That is

Facing:
The meticulous care lavished on the maintenance of the castle's interior comes from Countess Anna Provana di Collegno. Her family inherited the property from a cousin, Alessandro di Roero, who died without issue in 1898. The photograph shows a charming corner of the *Galleria Nuova*.

Left:
A view of the *Salottino Cinese*. The original eighteenth-century upholstery and hangings were manufactured by the East India Company and brought to Guarene directly from London.

Below:
The rich furnishings and decoration in the castle's rooms reaches a peak of extravagance in the *Stanza del Vescovo* (Bishop's Room). Elegant, French-inspired grotesques offset the *bandera* embroidery of the upholstery of the seatings and the canopy over the bed, a Louis Quatorze *lit à la duchesse*.

count. This noblewoman, who lives there with her family, is quick to proclaim her great love for Guarene, the "place of our roots."

It is she who now devotedly looks after the ancestral home, protecting its architectural and artistic heritage while also taking care of the extensive, extremely valuable archive that documents so much of the area's history. Thus continues the precious thread of civilization that has, fortunately, never been broken over the centuries.

magnificently sad). The rooms at Guarene rehearse a series of other classical motifs in the art—and *art de vivre*—of eighteenth-century Piedmont, against the backdrop of the triumph and subsequent rapid decline of absolutism in Europe. Passing the vast main staircase and going beyond the entrance hall, the visitor comes to the dining room and gallery, which reveal airy stuccoes, illusionistic ornamental frescoes, and sumptuous furnishings that have survived the passage of time. The *Stanza del Vescovo*, or Bishop's Room, reveals yet further evidence of the eighteenth century's refined decorative verve in the valuable and very colorful *bandera* embroidery embellishing the hangings and drapes. The Roero di Vezza e Guarene line became extinct when Count Alessandro died without heir in 1899 and Guarene passed to his cousin, Francesco Saverio Provana di Collegno, scion of another distinguished Piedmontese family whose history was closely bound up with that of the Savoys. The direct line of the Provana family also became extinct in the nineteenth century with Luisa, daughter of the ninth count, Alessandro, and Daria Bertone of the counts of Sambuy. The title then passed to the cadet branch, represented today by Anna Provana di Collegno, daughter of the thirteenth

PALAZZO BORROMEO

LAKE MAGGIORE
LOMBARDY

Facing, below, and following pages:
Aerial views of Isola Bella showing the *palazzo* complex, the small harbor, and the superb gardens. Work on the layout began when the noted architect, Giovanni Angelo Crivelli, was commissioned by Carlo III Borromeo in the seventeenth century. The challenging task of creating the terraces and trellises for the hanging garden was assigned to master mason Bartolomeo Scarione.

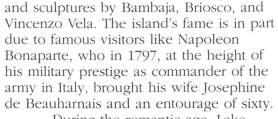

Isola Bella floats on Lake Maggiore like an enormous ship, with the truncated pyramid of the terraced garden in the south part making the stern, and its prow formed by the quay that extends in front of the monumental bulk of Palazzo Borromeo. Visitors to the island are struck by the seamless fusion of past and present. There is a satisfying sense of continuity, history, and noble, illustrious ancestral traditions that have managed, astoundingly, to endure.

The riot of spectacular baroque fantasy offers stunning, fairy-tale gardens, rare plants and woods, sixteenth-century Brussels tapestries, stuccoes, brocade wall hangings, valuable furnishings, and rooms that take their names from the celebrated artists who created them for the Borromeos. The works still conserved here are flanked by paintings by Moretto, *Il Cerano* (Giovanni Battista Crespi), and Luca Giordano, portraits by Cittadini, Salomon Adler, and Giuseppe Molteni,

and sculptures by Bambaja, Briosco, and Vincenzo Vela. The island's fame is in part due to famous visitors like Napoleon Bonaparte, who in 1797, at the height of his military prestige as commander of the army in Italy, brought his wife Josephine de Beauharnais and an entourage of sixty.

During the romantic age, Lake Maggiore became an obligatory, Baedeker-approved, port of call for the new wave of English-speaking visitors to *Il Bel Paese*. In 1828, Stendhal claimed that Isola Bella was one of the loveliest spots in the world, concluding like one of his own literary heroes, *"C'est ici qu'il faut se brûler la cervelle"* (It is here that one should burn one's brain).

Isola Madre, known as Isola di San Vittore at the time of its purchase, was at once renamed Renata, after Renato I Borromeo, when it was acquired, in 1501, by the Borromeos. This leading family of Lombard nobles still owns the property, maintaining it, like the other ancestral Borromeo holdings, in superb condition. The Borromeos came to the island in the mid sixteenth century, but it was only in the following century that the first building work began, under Giulio Cesare III Borromeo, who died in 1638.

More of the island's surface area was built over by Carlo III, who desired a residence, the Casino. This was entrusted in 1631 to the master mason, Andrea Scarione. At the same time, work began on the ambitious terracing and supports for the hanging garden, lending the island its characteristic, ziggurat-style profile. In the meantime, the island's name had been changed as a tribute to the owner's wife, Isabella d'Adda. Rechristened Isola Isabella, its new title would later be contracted to Isola Bella, or the Beautiful Island.

Carlo III, son of Renato I and Ersilia Farnese from the duchy of Parma, revived the family's fortunes after a period of political crisis. Borromeo faced fierce opposition from, among others, his uncle Federico, the cardinal made famous by

Manzoni, founder of Milan's Biblioteca Ambrosiana and the leading advocate of the canonization of his celebrated cousin, Carlo, his predecessor as archbishop of the Lombard capital. Carlo Borromeo, the champion of the triumphant Counter-Reformation, was portrayed by "his" artists, Cerano and Morazzone, as an emaciated figure, constantly fasting or mortifying the flesh, or bringing succor to plague victims during the terrible epidemic from 1576 to 1577. Carlo was canonized at Saint Peter's in the Vatican on November 1, 1610, when his cult and fame as a miracle worker were already widespread in Italy and beyond. In many respects, Federico was Carlo's creature. He became a cardinal in 1587 at the age of twenty-three. During his sojourn at Bologna under the protection of Cardinal Paleotti, and later in Rome at the Giustiniani household, he formed a deep passion for the arts. Nevertheless, Federico's career as cardinal and shepherd of the Milanese clergy did not get off to the best of starts. An exquisitely baroque clash with the Spaniards over the seat that should be reserved for the

governor in the duomo broke out when he arrived in Milan, and degenerated into a series of armed clashes. Tempers subsequently cooled. A collector of paintings, Federico also wrote a treatise entitled *De Pictura* (On Painting) and accumulated works by Dutch masters, especially Jan "Velvet" Bruegel and Paul Bril. He also bought the extraordinary *Basket of Fruit* by Caravaggio, an artist who, like the prelate, was from Lombardy.

But the real creator and guiding hand behind the *palazzo* and gardens on Isola Bella was Vitaliano VI, a military

commander of note in the French-Spanish war of 1647 to 1648, and in subsequent campaigns until 1659, when the Treaty of the Pyrenees re-established peace. For thirty years, Vitaliano devoted his time and energies to the project of transforming Isola Bella into the family sanctuary and garden of delights. Celebration of the Borromeo dynasty is explicit in the colossal statue of the family unicorn, and in the heraldic emblems scattered among the greenery, such as the motto *"humilitas"* in Gothic lettering. Completion of the entire project dragged on over the centuries and through a number of later interventions, all documented in the voluminous family archives. It was Vitaliano who decided to forgo the planned construction of the *casino*, so as not to lose the "flat and spacious" area of the garden.

The architect Francesco Castelli designed the monumental northern facade of the *palazzo*, which would be enhanced with porticoes and scenographic staircases. Inside, he brought the complex to life with the chapel, a theater, featuring graceful "half-moon" boxes, and the design for the gallery built in 1674 and known today as the *Galleria degli Arazzi*. Castelli's architectural project also reveals his intention to create a series of ground-floor rooms in the form of grottoes, inspired by the Mannerist *nymphaeum* at Lainate and built in 1689 by the architect Filippo Cagnola. Vitaliano VI Borromeo devoted much time and energy to the decoration and enhancement of the residence with paintings and other ornaments, as visitors may still observe in the *Sala delle Medaglie* (Medal Room), the *Sala del Trono* (Throne Room), or the *Sala delle Due Alcove* (Room of the Two Alcoves), also known as the *Sala della Regina* (Queen's Room). He hired an army of stuccoists, cabinetmakers, decorative painters, and figurative artists, including Federico Bianchi, Carlo Francesco Nuvolone, and Giovan Cristoforo Storer, in addition to celebrated landscape artists, such as the Dutchman Pieter Muller, known as *Cavalier Tempesta*, who painted nearly eighty works in the *palazzo*. Other artists also contributed, including flower and still-life specialists like Giovanni Saglier.

From 1671, Castelli was replaced by the architect Andrea Biffi, who worked there until his death in 1686. This ensured continuity for the only partially completed designs of the earlier supervisor. The meeting point of the residence and the garden, which are not in line, was disguised with a polygonal atrium. The monumental great staircase and basket-vault portico with its ashlar pillars were erected in the Piazza dell'Artiglieria, from which there is access to the *palazzo*. From 1677, Biffi elaborated the project "of the new quarter facing Isola Superiore," which was to take shape on the northwestern side in a series of high-profile reception rooms and a new gallery, now known as the *Galleria del*

barocchetto idiom, and of the mosaics in the *Sale delle Grotte* rooms. Francesco Zuccarelli was a Tuscan artist commissioned by Renato III Borromeo to complete seven canvases for the "room of the alcove in the new apartment." Zuccarelli delivered the works in person in October 1750. Giberto V Borromeo was an eminent politician during the days of the declining Ancien Régime, the rise of Napoleon, and the restoration. Equally committed both socially and culturally, Giberto was an enthusiastic supporter of the neoclassical idiom. We owe to him the acquisition of the three superb Renaissance monuments, Borromeo, Longhignana and Birago, redeemed at Milan at the time of the suppression of

Generale Berthier. There remained to be solved the question of the huge *Salone Centrale,* for which no satisfactory proposal could be formulated even after Biffi had consulted the great Gianlorenzo Bernini himself, the man whose vulcanic imagination had transformed the cityscape of baroque Rome. Debate on the *Salone* continued to rage, and the eminent Carlo Fontana was also enlisted. The plan was intended to hinge on four gigantic pillars supporting the dome above, drawing inspiration from the church of San Lorenzo in Milan. Arguments continued after the death of Vitaliano VI in 1690, when work was halted at the level of the tambour of the dome.

The eighteenth century witnessed the completion of the decoration in the

ecclesiastical properties and placed in the new chapel that Andrea Pizzala erected 1842 to 1844, modifying an earlier construction by Giuseppe Zanoja dating from 1789 to 1790. He was also responsible for the *Sala delle Colonne* (Column Room), or *Sala da Ballo* (Ballroom), the austere stables on the mainland opposite the quay, and the *Rotonda* in the garden. The garden acquired its present configuration between 1631 and 1671, first at the initiative of Carlo III Borromeo and under the supervision of Giovanni Angelo Crivelli, who completed the terraces of the *soprascoglio* (clifftop), arranging citrus plants and vegetables in a sort of geometric herb garden. Later, Francesco Castelli's abundant verve and imagination

added spires, pyramids, and obelisks in *migliarolo,* a local granite, and a vast crowd of statues. The hand that guided the intervention belonged to Cardinal Giberto, who was prodigal with advice and suggestions to his brother Vitaliano. In 1666, grottoes were created on the ground where the chapel of San Rocco stood. The following year, work was under way on the *Teatro delle Commedie* and the *Teatro delle Fontane.*

In the meantime, the iconographic program was developing around two key themes. The heraldic glorification of the noble house culminated in the spectacular *Teatro Massimo,* the highest point on the island, dominated by the Borromeo unicorn. This was complemented by an allegorical dimension that exalted the concepts of nature and artifice. In 1734, Vincenzo Elia Buzzi sculpted a colossal Diana for the "laurel grove" and Grazioso Rusca added further sculptures in 1790. In the early nineteenth century, the new hothouses were erected and the lake water pumping system, created in 1672 with the help of Gian Maria Mora, Clement IX's *fontanaro,* or water engineer, was also modernized. From 1819, Count Vitaliano IX Borromeo graced the garden with many unusual exotic plants, planting in the "Terrace of Plants from New Holland" a celebrated camphor laurel, palm trees, rare conifers from New Zealand, camellias, azaleas, and the Malabar jasmine.

VILLA
FONTANELLE
(VERSACE)
LAKE COMO
LOMBARDY

"The horticultural inheritance at the Villa Fontanelle on Lake Como was a splendid one, for it had been planted a century ago in the naturalistic English manner with superb specimen trees, some of whose branches sweep downward to touch the waters of the lake. The land rises sharply at the back of the villa, accessible by means of winding paths and flights of steps that ascend its rocky surface from which trees soar upward and down which mountain streams gush. Those waters have proved a great gift to the garden, for they have brought animation in the form of a grotto, cascades, and a fountain. But when I first came a decade ago these elements looked tired and lay like some Sleeping Beauty to be awakened. I recall sitting by the faded dusty parterre, which stretches out like a carpet beneath the facade that faces the lake, making some scribbles suggesting what might be done.

On the next visit our bedroom window was flung wide and Gianni Versace said, 'There, Roy, is your garden.' Well, that was not quite true because it was Versace's own garden transformed by the application of his own imagination. In the years that have followed, I have watched that garden change and grow. White lilies arise from a sparkling fountain in the midst of what is now an immaculate parterre, but they have multiplied with others added beneath two other facades. Medusa wall fountains spout water framed by an ivy-clad arcade in the center of which Neptune wields his trident against a curtain of cascading water. Everywhere statues have sprung up and a small army of gods and goddesses populate the hillside. Urns bearing trophies of shiny evergreens punctuate walks or march along the balustrade next to the lake. A river god reclines amidst ferns presiding

52

over a sinuous design of baroque scrolls etched in pebbles and verdant turf. One sees the classical taste that animates the interior spill out through and across the garden. One witnesses too, in the vivid swathes of purple pansies or pink begonias that fill the parterres, Versace's unashamed delight in the use of strong color."

It looks like a fairy tale, measured off in distant, joyful images and floating in the suspended, dream-like dimension of a radiantly happy, unreachable world. Yet this enchanted garden, resuscitated as if by magic from neglect and the ravages of time, actually exists. And who better to describe it than one of its creators, Sir Roy Strong, the garden designer favored by Queen Elizabeth II, former director of the Victoria and Albert Museum, and conscientious consultant for the restoration of the park after Villa Fontanelle was acquired by Gianni Versace, in 1977. Gianni Versace, as a native of Magna

Above:
A small corridor with paintings portraying three dancing Muses. On the right of the photograph is a marble Hebe in the style of Canova.

Below:
A reception room. The walls are decorated with trompe l'oeil vases of ivy and pillars. By the door is a reproduction of the celebrated bronze tripod from Pompeii.

Grecia, was entranced by beauty. In love with the classical ideal of beauty, he devoted his life to its pursuit and fell in love with the villa at first sight. It was a *coup de foudre*, symptomatic of a mysterious yearning for continuity, for roots at last regained after being sought out with tenacity and profound affection. "This is my real home," Versace liked to say. "It is a place of the spirit, where the family gathers together at Christmas . . . in short, it is the house of Bergman's films, the place you end up coming back to. . . ." Even today, Versace's presence is perceptible in the villa's rooms. His powerful creative stamp, endless curiosity about the human condition, and amazing energy are still vibrantly evident, reassuring, enfolding, and exciting visitors.

Villa Fontanelle was built in the romantic period, when an eccentric English lord, Charles Currie, fell in love with Lake Como. Unable to find a property to purchase, he bought a disused quarry where once *pietra moltrasina* stone had been extracted. The purchase took place in the mid nineteenth century, when Lake Como, with its magnificent residences and flower-bedecked gardens, was a must-visit destination for visitors from northern Europe as they headed south. Currie hired *comballi*, large sailing vessels with a single square sail, to transport enormous quantities of soil to the quarry, creating a wood in which he laid out paths that crisscrossed the property and joined the Via Regina highway, thought to date back to the Lombard queen, Theodolinda. He made the carriage road leading from the Via Regina almost to the lakeside.

Lord Currie built a home for the estate guardian and gardener where the estate borders on the Via Regina. He also erected a small edifice lower down, in the open area at the end of the carriage road, then called *Il Palazzetto*, so he could supervise work on the larger house he was building as his personal residence. The year was 1865 and the Victorian age was at its height. The mysterious Lord Currie spent many years in his new villa, even acquiring Italian nationality in addition to his British citizenship. An enthusiast of Darwin and the new frontiers of science, Currie fervently sought the reconciliation of humanity with the forces of nature. To further his quest, he spent whole days stark naked in the villa's grounds, sheltered by its thick hedges and high perimeter walls from prying eyes and the scandal that his naturist inclinations would have provoked in his more conventional neighbors.

Above and below:
It was Gianni Versace's wish that Villa Fontanelle should be restored to Lord Currie's original plans. Below is a detail of the frame of the mirror over the fireplace.

The villa stands on the steep mountainside that descends to the waters of the lake, which is how it appears in a nineteenth-century print. It is a plain, parallelepiped building, with elegant classical lines, surmounted by a graceful turret. An attractive pavilion, with painted Gothic troubadour-style decoration, was erected to the left of the main building. It was followed by an exotic note struck by the fantastic oriental gazebo mirrored in the lake, observing the passage of the typical Lake Como boats and the more elaborate full dress vessels of the nobility, complete with canopy and liveried oarsmen. Further up the slope on the extreme right of the garden, there is a small neo-Gothic *folie*.

In 1873, Lord Currie put his estate on the market as suddenly as he had acquired it, for no apparent reason. In the eighteenth and nineteenth centuries, Lake Como was a favorite resort of European high society, who mingled there with leading families from the local aristocracy and Milan's fast-rising middle classes. Before it was converted into a celebrated hotel, the sixteenth-century Villa d'Este was acquired in the early nineteenth century, by Princess Caroline of Brunswick—the estranged and scandal-clouded consort of the equally extro-verted British Prince Regent—passing next to the Czarina of Russia. A short distance from Villa Fontanelle is Villa Erba, then Villa Visconti di Modrone. The new owner of Villa Fontanelle, whose name was Antonio Besana, was from Lombardy. Besana resided there for most of the year, earning merit as a philanthropist, for he provided the village of Moltrasio with a modern water supply system at his own expense. To the music of the popular song *Bela Gigogin* and the dazzling stage show *Ballo Excelsior*, Cavalier Besana, a personal friend of Giuseppe Verdi set up the local village band, paying for their instruments himself, while positivism and industrial progress made headway in the foggy Po Valley and the Italy of the Savoys began to find its feet. Besana, who never married, left the villa to his brother Giovanni, his father's son by a second marriage and forty years his junior.

In 1911, the property passed from Giovanni Besana to his daughter, Fanny, who had married Angelo Marietti. From 1917 to 1931 there was a further inheritance favoring Fanny's four heirs, Eugenia, Lina, Alfonso, and Paolina—names that seem to have leapt from the pages of a verismo novel or a work from the Lombard *Scapigliatura* literary movement. In 1931, Alfonso married and became the new owner of the castle, as well as part of the village of Cerennio Plinio in the upper part of Lake Como. His sisters did not wish to keep the house at Moltrasio and decided to sell it to the noble Cambiaghi family of bankers from Milan. When Gianni Versace arrived, Villa Fontanelle was in a lamentable state of decay. No one had lived in the property

for any length of time since 1942. The building itself may have looked tarnished but the garden had been allowed to run wild and to become an impenetrable jungle. A sorcerer's spell had wiped away its avenues, parterres, fountains, and hedges. Trees and bushes were smothered by the advancing undergrowth's embrace. Inside the villa itself, only scattered fragments remained of the once extensive mosaic floorings. The eclectic mural paintings by late nineteenth-century artists from Como were coming away from the damp-swollen, mold-covered walls. Gianni Versace, however, took all this in his stride. He could sense that everything would be restored to its former splendor and that he would be at home here as

nowhere else in the world. Jealous of his new treasure, and determined to scrupulously respect the villa's original spirit, Versace set out to do all the work on his own, without help from architects or interior designers. With infinite patience, he found Lord Currie's original plans and, having selected a superbly qualified team to carry out the restoration program, Versace then contacted Sir Roy Strong, a world authority on the subject, to act as his special consultant for the recovery of the garden. The effort required a full decade. The garden now leads the visitor to the house, which presents a solemn entrance hall watched over by four neoclassical statues portraying the four Platonic virtues, Fortitude, Prudence, Temperance, and

Justice. More neoclassical statues peek out of niches on the long marble staircase that leads to the upper floors. At the end of a long corridor, we come to the *salone d'onore*, or main hall, with its fine collection of neoclassical Milanese, German, and Neapolitan paintings. In the dining room, there are sculptures and paintings by Giuliano Traballesi and Andrea Appiani.

The villa is a hymn to European neoclassicism and the movement's sophisticated atmosphere of attenuated, yet opulent, elegance. The list of artists represented is a roll call of emblematic names, including Mengs, Volpato, Sablet, Valadier, Thomire, Jacob, Percier, Fontaine, Jacques-Louis David, Luigi Canonica, and Giocondo Albertolli. One of the three large bedrooms on the first floor contains a display of canvases, watercolors, and sketches of stage sets by Luigi Ademollo, a leading figure in the neoclassical movement. Ademollo, born

in Milan in 1764, took up painting after making a detailed study of classical antiquity, which he rounded off in the Rome of Canova, Goethe, and the Grand Tour. Hired in 1788, when he was just over twenty, to work on the paintings for Florence's Teatro degli Immobili, Ademollo was later to leave that city his masterly frescoes and decorations in the Palatine Chapel and in various rooms at Palazzo Pitti for Grand Duke Ferdinando III of Lorraine, as well as in Palazzo Pucci and Palazzo Capponi, inventing his own "expressionist" version of neoclassicism. He was an ideal spiritual companion for Gianni Versace, illuminated by the same atavistic aspiration to beauty, and by an identical, absolute rapture for the lost paradise of classical antiquity.

VILLA
BETTONI CAZZAGO

LAKE GARDA
LOMBARDY

Lake Garda was a favorite destination for eighteenth-century northern European travelers arriving in the Mediterranean to savor the soul of classicism, Johann Gottfried Herder and Johann Wolfgang Goethe, to name but two. This deep imprint is still evident today, *mutatis* *mutandis* (with the necessary changes). Sirmione, home of the Roman poet, Caius Valerius Catullus, emerges in its almost marine beauty in the nostalgic lyrical poetry that the Latin writer composed in the first century before Christ. The rhythmically rippling blue of Lake Garda that German Grand Tourists were finally able to see when they emerged from the rocky spurs at Nago seemed to herald the arrival of a new, different dawn, and the invigorating ancestral life blood of the classical world. However, sixteenth-century Veronese nobles steeped in

Above:
One of the statues that adorn the balustrade of the building.

Facing and far upper right:
Work on Villa Bettoni began in 1750, after the architect Adriano Cristofoli had been commissioned by Giandomenico Bettoni. Today, the villa can be considered the most important example of eighteenth-century sponsored architecture on Lake Garda.

classical culture and the Petrarchian mindset revived in the early years of the century by the sophisticated intellectual circle that gathered on the Asolo hills. Caterina Cornaro, queen of Cyprus, was at the center of the group that, under the patronage of Pietro Bembo, had learned to appreciate Benaco as the ideal setting for refined *otia*, or literary diversions. For example, Agostino Brenzone, the illustrious jurisconsult and philosopher, began to construct his own lakeside *delizia*, or pleasure lodge, in 1538 at Punta San Vigilio, commissioning the plans from the innovative architect, Michele Sanmicheli. The huge collection of classical antiquities and the crisply regular perfection of the countryside, create an inimitable, absolute magic. Quite apart from the hordes of tourists who today, particularly in summer, crowd

the lovely old towns and pretty resorts that surround the largest of Italy's lakes, there is another, secret, and especially fascinating Garda—the Garda of ancient aristocratic villas and their gardens. One of the most significant parks is the perspective garden of Villa Bettoni Cazzago at Bogliaco, near Gargnano, on the Brescia shore of the lake. It was already described in the eighteenth century as "the loveliest thing in all Lombardy" and its magnificently scenic original layout has remained intact.

Bogliaco's attractive narrow lakeside lanes offer art and architecture that mix very different periods, lemon groves, and delightful views in an austere, mountainous setting. The village, administratively part of Gargnano lies on the road to Riva del Garda that was opened in 1931, interrupting the centuries-old isolation of the upper part of the lake. Gabriele d'Annunzio, who had installed himself at nearby Vittoriale degli Italiani, called it the "meander," for its "concealed and tortuous" route penetrating to the very heart of the mountain.

As we have seen, villas and pleasure lodges began to be built on the

Above:
A glimpse of the layout of the garden, inspired by the theatrical scenographies of the Galli da Bibbiena family.

shores of Italy's great lakes in the sixteenth century. They were centers for farming and various other economic activities of an aristocracy that was investing increasingly heavily in land and extending its commercial interests with equal alacrity. These were utilitarian centers of production that also served as congenial places of residence, as Stendhal wrote, referring to the villas built in Brianza by Milanese nobles, which were "too much to call *palazzi*, and too little to call country houses." Villa Bettoni is indisputably the finest example of eighteenth-century private architecture on Lake Garda. The late Lombard Baroque vocabulary of the residential edifice, reined in by an influence that goes back to Palladio, precedes that neoclassical movement that gained popularity in the late eighteenth century. It takes on freer, more scenic connotations in the layout of the garden behind. The Veronese architect, Adriano Cristofoli, was commissioned by Giandomenico Bettoni and began building work around 1750.

There are two extended, and relatively similar, frontages. One, solemn and compact, looks onto the lake and the other facade, higher and of more complicated design, opens onto the garden. Today, it is separated from the residential section by the main highway, dating from the 1930s. The construction comprises three floors on a rusticated ashlar ground level broken up by Corinthian *lesenes* and light moldings. In the center, the *piano nobile* flaunts three large apertures topped by broken-apex pediments that frame round niches with marble busts. The double staircase of the

landward facade denotes an effort to achieve greater monumentality of design in linking house and garden, in comparison with the composition of the lakeside front. A balustrade with urns and statues adorns the upper part of the building, heralding the magnificent prospect of the terraced garden that unfolds on the slope behind. The monumental staircase inside also has an impressive scenic impact. It extends from the colonnaded entrance hall designed by Antonio Marchetti, a disciple of Cristofoli and his successor as supervisor of works at the villa. The gaggle of allegorical and mythologically-inspired statues atop the balustrade engages in a dialogue with the illusionistic frescoes of brothers Bernardino and Fabrizio Galliari, hired in 1761 and active here until the following year. They also contributed to the fresh rocaille decor of the vast ball room on the second floor, giving full flight to their imagination in a joyous riot of garlands, playful *putti*, medallions, moldings, consoles, capricious cornices, niches, shells, and curving trompe l'oeil pediments. The dining room is from the seventeenth century and predates the Cristofolis' makeover. The ceiling is

frescoed with illusionistic architectural motifs and on the walls hang eight large paintings by the Venetian artist, Andrea Celesti. The superb, elaborate gilt wood frames contain episodes from Roman and Asian history. Raised passages take you from the villa to the Italian garden, laid out to a design by Amerigo Vincenzo Pierallini between 1764 and 1767.

While the exquisitely eighteenth-century leitmotiv of the interior at Villa Bettoni is its dazzling ceremonial formality, and studiedly sumptuous theatricality, the garden takes this vocation to its logical conclusion in a *chef d'oeuvre* of unashamedly dramatic impact. As in one of the extraordinary deceptive baroque backdrops that the Galliari da Bibbiena family created in the seventeenth and eighteenth centuries for operas and theatrical performances, and to amaze the courts of Europe, the garden at Villa Bettoni draws on the ambitiously imaginative use of perspective. The scenic machine artfully expands the visual approach, exploiting the various levels of the terraces, the pediments, the niches, the obelisks, and the allegorical sculptures in white Torri marble. The unexpected, fascinating, challenge to the observer's eye opens up endless, imaginary dimensions, created according to the very baroque vision of *maraviglia* (wonder) and *movimento* (movement)—"the soul of all the world is but movement," claimed the French poet Motin in the mid seventeenth century. The strong vertical thrust conjures up, starting from the bottom, a curious illusionistic effect. It cancels out the horizontal extension of the garden's very distinctive terraces, whose full breadth can only be grasped from above.

PALAZZO DUCALE
MANTUA, LOMBARDY

Sheltered on three sides by the waters of the four lakes formed by the Mincio, at least until the eighteenth century, when Lake Paiolo was drained, Mantua was also protected by imposing defences. A veritable fortress, the city was for long considered impregnable. From 1272, Mantua was firmly in the hands of the Bonacolsi family, but in 1328, the tables were turned in a single night when their rivals, Gonzagas, gained supremacy. It was August 16, 1328 and the humidity must have lain heavy on the wet, mosquito-plagued flatlands as the Gonzaga's troops chased their enemies from Mantua to take possession of the buildings between the *Duomo* and what is today Via Accademia, the headquarters of the Bonacolsi faction. A bloodbath

ensued. According to the traditional story, the last of the Bonacolsis—Rinaldo, known as *Il Passerino*—was put to the sword by Francesco Gonzaga himself. The corpse had been embalmed and placed by the victors on top of a hippopotamus as a *Wunderkammer* curiosity. The Bonacolsi son, Francesco, suffered an even worse fate, for he was shut up in a tower of Castellaro, today's Castel d'Ario, until he died. Since then, Mantua has had its glories and its darker days, but it has remained indissolubly linked to the Gonzaga dynasty.

From their beginnings as a family of wealthy landowners, the Gonzagas rose to become leading actors on the European stage by making shrewd matrimonial alliances with various royal houses. After the family obtained in 1433 the hereditary title of marquis from Emperor Sigismund, there followed four centuries of brilliance, ushered in by Ludovico II, the *signore*, or lord, of Mantua from 1444 to 1478. It was he who inaugurated the marvelous Mantuan Renaissance. Ludovico II was the first to realize the power of propaganda, and the immense prestige that could be derived from the nascent Renaissance culture and the flourishing of the arts. For a state without significant economic influence, and in a well-defended, but strategically dangerous position amid much more powerful neighbors, the arts were a crucial resource. The marquis, assisted by

Above:
A bust of Federico II Gonzaga, under whom the family acquired their ducal title and Monferrato. On his death in 1540, Federico was succeeded by his son, Francesco III. The bust is in the *Appartamento della Guastalla.*

Below:
The *Appartamento degli Arazzi* comprises three main rooms and a smaller chamber. It provides a suitable display space for rich tapestries illustrating the Acts of the Apostles.

Facing:
The *Salone degli Specchi,* or Mirror Room, takes its name from the huge mirrors put there by Giocondo Albertolli in 1779, in conformity with neoclassical tastes.

seventeenth centuries, when the family's fortunes (by then represented by the French cadet branch of Gonzaga Nevers) went into a swift and inexorable decline. The *palazzo "in forma di città"* (in the shape of a city) was a vast labyrinth of rooms, gardens, loggias, and apartments that the various members of the house had insisted on adding.

The Gonzaga duchy was a bellwether state in the dangerous military and political game that set Venice against Milan. Tenacious, gloomy, and romantic in disposition, the dukes could be thrifty to the point of avarice. Their decline was swift and irreversible, as Montesquieu relates. In late July 1729, the French philosopher visited the melancholy halls of the palace, then the residence of the Hapsburg governor, only twenty-two years after the death of the last, unwarlike duke of Mantua, Ferdinando Carlo Gonzaga Nevers. But the decline was obvious much earlier and can be traced to the years 1627 and 1628. That was when the superb art collection, assembled by the Gonzagas over centuries of passionate connoisseurship, was in large part sold by the last duke from the family's main branch, Vincenzo II, through the Flemish merchant Daniel Nys to Charles I Stuart, the Catholic king of England. The second, ruinous, wound inflicted on the living flesh of this

his wife, Barbara of Brandenburg, tirelessly wove a masterly fabric of diplomatic relations. He managed to obtain from Pius II a cardinalate for his eighteen-year-old son, Francesco, projecting Mantua onto the great stage of European politics. From May 27, 1459 to January 19, 1460, the city hosted the diet called by the pope to launch a new crusade against the Turks, who in 1453 had conquered Constantinople, putting an end to the Eastern Roman Empire.

An excellent administrator, shrewd statesman, and generous patron, Ludovico attracted to Mantua the finest artists and intellectuals of the day, from Leon Battista Alberti (who designed for the city two of his finest churches, Sant'Andrea and San Sebastiano) to Luca Fancelli, Donatello, Luciano Laurana, and Andrea Mantegna.

Palazzo Ducale has been the name of the building since 1530, when Charles V Hapsburg promoted the loyal supporter of the empire, Marquis Federico II Gonzaga, to the rank of duke. A huge building covering about eight-and-a-half acres, Palazzo Ducale was constructed between the late twelfth and mid

Renaissance monument, and on the collective memory of Mantua itself, was the sack of the town by the *Landsknechts* of the imperial armies in 1630 and 1631, when much of what remained was destroyed and dispersed. From that moment on, Charles of Nevers, who had risen to the duchy on marrying his cousin, Maria Gonzaga, would have other worries that were more pressing than art collections as he struggled to stay afloat in the tumultuous flood of the politics of the day. All those who were involved in the ill-advised sale came to a sad end. Vincenzo II died shortly afterwards, hated by his fellow citizens for desecrating the city's artistic heritage, Nys died a pauper, and Charles I was beheaded by the Parliamentarians in 1649.

A recent, very impressive, exhibition entitled *La Celeste Galeria*, held at Palazzo Ducale and Palazzo Te, attempted to piece together, as far as

possible, the map of the Gonzaga palace treasures. Paintings by Mantegna, Giulio Romano, Correggio, Titian, Lorenzo Lotto, Dosso Dossi, Tintoretto, Lucas Cranach, Federico Barocci, Domenico Fetti, Guercino, Domenichino, Guido Reni, and Pieter Paul Rubens, the artist particularly admired by Vincenzo I, were joined by the superb bronzes of Antico, the elegant, classically inspired sculptor in the service of the marquess, Isabella, and of Giambologna. There were also classical statues and reliefs, including those that

once belonged to Andrea Mantegna, valuable musical instruments, weapons, tapestries, rock crystal engravings by the Saracchis, as well as medals and ancient cameos mounted in the supremely whimsical mannerist fashion.

Palazzo Ducale reveals the genius of the Gonzagas as patrons, as much as it does the skills of the artists who worked there, from Bartolino da Novara, Pisanello, Andrea Mantegna, and the great Giulio Romano. Contributions also came from Pompeo Pedemonte, creator of the huge "hanging garden" and Bernardino Facciotto, who in 1580 and 1581 built the "eight-sided courtyard," also known as *degli Orsi*, or "of the Bears." Bernardino Brugnoli and Giovan Angelo Barbassolo continued Pedemonte's work on the "hanging garden" and Fra' Zenobio Bocchi in 1603 laid out the "garden of simple plants," with its many medicinal herbs. The most ancient part of the *palazzo* comprises the buildings on Piazza Sordello, the Magna Domus, and

the apartments of Corte Nuova and the Palazzina della Rustica. In the course of the sixteenth century, Giovan Battista Bertani, prefect of the ducal buildings, was the focus of a far-reaching program of restructuring and extension, including the Basilica Palatina di Santa Barbara, the court church, which has a distinct vocation for music.

The last major building projects were conducted by Antonio Maria Viani, whose precious, rigidly magniloquent architectural and decorative idiom bridges the sixteenth and seventeenth centuries in the apartments of Vincenzo I, the *Sale delle Metamorfosi* and the *Loggia di Eleonora*. Finally, under the Austrian domination in the eighteenth century, when the dynasty had become extinct, Paolo Pozzo carried out essential repair and restoration work.

There is something extreme, and even pathological, about the Gonzagas' impulse for patronage and collecting art. The prestige of the family and the

the Palazzo del Capitano, which date back to the Bonacolsis. In the late fourteenth century, Bartolino da Novara erected the Castello di San Giorgio and a hundred years later, Luca Fancelli built the Renaissance Domus Nova.

The dazzling brilliance of Giulio Romano in the 1520s and the impact of mannerism enhanced the new buildings at the Palazzina della Paleologa, unfortunately subsequently destroyed, and

Above:
A fine view of the *Galleria dei Marmi*.

Facing:
Detail of a second century A.D. Roman sarcophagus in the *Appartamento di Troia*, located in the part of the palace known as *Corte Nuova*, which was designed by Giulio Romano in the sixteenth century.

Facing:
The west wall of the *Camera degli Sposi* depicts the meeting on January 1, 1462 of Ludovico II Gonzaga and his sons Federico and Francesco, just after his election by Pius II as the first cardinal from the house of Gonzaga.

political idea of defending its power and independence were symbolized by cultural supremacy. This was true both in the early, humanist days of the Gonzagas' rise to power and, in the last, bitter days of their downward trajectory, when the generous, brilliant Vincenzo I, the patron of Monteverdi and a ruler who identified himself with the heroes of Ariosto and Torquato Tasso, squandered his own life and Mantua's riches in a vain struggle to reassert the family's importance in a Europe rent apart by the conflict between France and Spain. Other Gonzagas were extraordinary Renaissance figures, like Ludovico II and the brilliant Isabella d'Este, mistress of the celebrated carved and inlaid *Studiolo*, decorated with paintings by Mantegna, Lorenzo Costa, Lorenzo Leombruno, and Pietro Perugino, as well as the equally famous *grotta*, which housed 1,600 antiquities and valuable objects. Ludovico commissioned the *Camera Picta* or *Camera degli Sposi* (Painted Room or Bride and Groom's Room) at the Castello di San Giorgio, which was probably completed by Andrea Mantegna between 1465 and 1474. The marquis and his artist shared a true friendship, as is clear from the nobleman's reply to a certain Simone di Ardizzone, who had come to him to complain about Mantegna's arrogance. "I love the tip of this Andrea's foot more than a thousand ne'er-do-wells like you." *Opus Hoc Tenue* (*This Slender Work*) was how Mantegna referred to his masterpiece, a perfect example of the Renaissance spirit, inspired by a classical source, the poem *On A Room* by Lucian of Samosata. Mantegna treats the series of figures with a vigorous Lombard realism, that at times verges on cruelty; they jostle in front of crisply defined, metaphysical landscapes dotted with Roman details. We note the family of Ludovico and Barbara, whose progeny were to engender the cadet branches of the Gonzagas. We see the court dwarfs and Rubino, their favorite dog. There is also the Hapsburg emperor Frederick III Hapsburg and Christian I of Denmark, who came for the papal diet called to launch the crusade against the Ottomans. In the middle of the elaborate, coffered, illusionistic, *en grisaille*-decorated ceiling, with its *tondi* of Roman emperors, the balconied trompe l'oeil central aperture seems to open onto a

75

laughing, enchanted world lit by a bright, turquoise sky. Ludovico and Isabella would be followed by the brilliant, melancholic, Vincenzo I, who was preceded by his father, Guglielmo, and his sister Margherita, widow of Alfonso II of Este. In all, the Gonzagas were responsible for more than a century of passionate collecting. Yet it took only three years to scatter everything to the winds. Magnificence, morbidity, sensuality, and the Counter-Reformation, came together in a terrible dilemma for the family, torn between an outdated, Tassoesque outlook on life and the eighteenth-century pomp of courts torn apart by passionless struggles for power.

PALAZZO PISANI MORETTA
VENICE, VENETO

Facing:
The exotic facade of the *palazzo* overlooking the Grand Canal. Two pointed arch canal entrances set side by side tell us that there were once two separate households living here, although both belonged to the same family.

Below left:
A lovely view of one of the rooms on the *piano nobile*, or main floor. Note the rich crimson wall hangings and the eighteenth-century Venetian mirror and console table.

The eighteenth century, the glorious, spectacular final act in the long, historic and artistic saga of the Most Serene Republic, opened as Venice was regaining, after about a hundred years of relative obscurity, her leading role in the arts in Italy. At the same time, the city was sliding into a fatal political and economic dissolution. The curtain was lowered for the last time in 1797 by Napoleon Bonaparte. The magical, controversial Settecento was the century of rococo, of Canaletto, Bellotto, Guardi, and the masks that in Venice could be worn for several months a year, outside the traditional Carnival period. Masks instantly eliminated social distinctions and were de rigueur for nobles, splendidly costumed courtesans, high-ranking clerics, and gallant ne'er-do-wells at the gaming table, as they feverishly squandered colossal fortunes in the public and privately owned *ridotti* and *casini*, the gambling houses to be found all over the city. The mask was midwife to political intrigue, and the ever-present accomplice of amorous adventures, consumed behind the curtains of Venice's bedrooms, gondolas, and even convents, as Giacomo Casanova's *Mémoires* reveal. The Most Serene Republic's weary *Grand Siècle* was a glittering, never-ending masked ball that attracted to the lagoon a steady stream of potentates, actors, intellectuals, and musicians from all over Europe. The Settecento commenced to the strains of Benedetto Marcello and Vivaldi, against the backdrop of paintings by Sebastiano Ricci, to be swept up in the exciting epic of Giambattista Tiepolo. His was an unrestrained, light-filled yet solemn art that combined plastic qualities with intangibility.

The melancholy, carefree Venice in decline, described by Longhi and Goldoni, shared ascendancy with Charles III's Naples over Europe's music scene. Venice's many theaters staged fully 1,274 operas and her various hospital institutions became workshops of musical

composition. No architect contrived to leave a lasting mark on the lagoon city during the eighteenth century. Venice remained faithful to Palladio, endlessly reworking his modules and insights. The interiors of the old and new aristocracy's *palazzi* were masterpieces of patrician magnificence, comfort and *savoir vivre*, proffering decorative schemes and furnishings of unrivaled pomp. Lavish stucco, brocades and damask silks, carved or lacquered furniture, glass chandeliers in spectacularly theatrical shapes, and a host of mirrors, large and small, contrived to create multiple illusionary scenic effects, opening as if by magic onto fantastical rooms, and scattering the blue-green waters of the canals with pleasing reflected images.

In the century of enlightenment, Palazzo Pisani Moretta, which stands on the Grand Canal near San Tomà, also underwent an extraordinary interior transformation. The quatrefoil tracery of the building's windows, which is characteristic of fifteenth-century Venetian architecture, recalls the design of the Doge's Palace. A typical example of the late Gothic style, the Palazzo Pisani Moretta passed to the Pisani family in May 1629, and was used as a permanent residence after 1670. The two pointed arch canal entrances, set side by side, tell us that the building's two *piani nobili* were used by two distinct households, both belonging to the same family. The curious name "Moretta" is thought to indicate that the building belonged to the branch of the Pisani family that descended from a certain Almorò, or Ermolao in the Venetian dialect, who lived in the fourteenth century. According

Following pages left to right:
Today, Palazzo Pisani Moretta is one of Venice's most complete and best conserved noble residences. The dining room has a remarkable collection of eighteenth-century Venetian porcelain.

The so-called *Sala Gialla*, or Yellow Room, on the *piano nobile*. The gilt vegetal curtain rail and the eighteenth-century Louis Seize chairs are especially interesting.

Facing and far right:
The transparent, multicolored Murano glass chandelier in this extravagantly decorated room was designed by the great Venetian glassmaker Briati in the eighteenth century. The frescoes on the ceiling are enhanced by *quadratura* decorations and illusionistic architectural perspectives.

Below:
The *pòrtego*, which was subsequently converted into a ballroom, features marble-effect Corinthian pillars alternating with white spiral-motif candelabra on a green background, fillets with gilt stucco garlands, and imposing mirrors. The Murano chandeliers and the airy fresco by Jacopo Guarana are also superb.

the Rocca Pisana at Lonigo, conceived by Palladio's leading disciple, Vincenzo Scamozzi.

The Venice *palazzo* of the Pisanis of San Polo, constructed in a graceful Gothic style at the beginning of the fifteenth century, reveals a rocaille decorative scheme of great sophistication. Today, as in the past, it is a venue for receptions and formal entertainments. In the nineteenth century, the building was acquired by the Giusti del Giardino family, when one of the three daughters of the noble Vettor Daniele Pisani married a scion of that noble Verona household. From them, Palazzo Pisani Moretta passed to the Counts Sammartini through Giulia Bianchini d'Alberigo, widow of Vettor Giusti. The Sammartinis continue to own the *palazzo* and have revived its somewhat tarnished splendor with patience and devoted attention, reassembling and ceaselessly enriching the original furnishings and fitments. The superb decorative scheme of the huge rooms on the first *piano nobile*, and of the smaller ones of the floor above, were commissioned by Chiara Pisani, the extremely wealthy daughter of the *procuratore*, or magistrate, Francesco, and last of the Moretta branch of the family. As the sole heir, Chiara inherited the *palazzo* and, from 1739 to 1743, began a radical and ambitious program to

to this theory, the *palazzo*'s name is a corrupt version of this ancestor's first name, distorted by repetition over the centuries. Almorò was also the founder of the Santo Stefano and Santa Maria Zobenigo branches of the Pisani family while, in the fourteenth century, Bertucci, the son of Nicolò, was the first member of the Pisani "dal Banco" branch of bankers and merchants. The noble Pisani family, whose roots originally lay in Tuscany, were enrolled in 1307 in the Maggior Consiglio in the person of Nicolò, whose long and prestigious career was closely bound up with that of Venice

itself. The Pisanis were to maintain their position in the first rank of the city's great patrician families. The degree of political and economic influence achieved by the Pisanis "da San Polo," perhaps the most distinguished of the branches that made up the family tree, is clear above all from the magnificent buildings they commissioned. We only have to remember the out-of-town *palagio* at Montagnana, not far from Padua, by Andrea Palladio, or the celebrated villa at Bagnolo, again designed by the great sixteenth-century architect. We could also mention the abstract neo-feudal design of

redecorate the interior of the building in the rococo idiom. Her sons, Vettor and Pietro Vettor, carried out further alterations that anticipated the burgeoning neoclassical movement in a series of interventions that began in 1770 to conclude in 1773.

Access to Palazzo Pisani Moretta is through the vast entrance hall on the first floor. The austere great staircase, created during the general modernization program promoted by the architect Andrea Tirali from 1739 to 1743, leads up to the *piano nobile*, its flights supported by composite columns. The *pòrtego*, the long living area arranged perpendicular to the course of the canals, is a typical feature of noble Venetian residences from the Gothic period. Here, the *pòrtego* has been converted into a magnificent reception hall. The progression of the walls is lively and eye-catching. Marble-effect Corinthian pillars alternate with tapering white spiral-motif candelabra on a green background and fillets with gilt stucco garlands. This astonishing fairy-tale decorative theme is further accentuated by four large mirrors and intricate shell ornaments over the door. The elaborate illusionistic *quadratura* decoration of the ceiling, frescoed by Jacopo Guarana in 1772, opens to reveal a blue, light-filled sky traversed by whirling clouds and crowded with agitated figures. A sumptuous succession of Murano chandeliers suffuses the room with the ancient light of its candles. In 1775, the *palazzo* was the subject of a legal battle whose endless coups de théâtre were the talk of all Venice, splitting the citizens into two opposing camps. Pietro Pisani was the issue of a relationship of Chiara Pisani's second child, Vettor, with a lowborn woman he later married in secret. On the death of his father, who married a Grimani after the ecclesiastical annulment of his first union, Pietro rekindled the scandal of his clandestine birth in a convent by publicly laying claim to his share of the estate. To the dismay of his stepsister Chiara and uncle, the *procuratore* Pietro Vettor, the young Pietro was awarded the Pisani estates at Montagnana, a number of properties in Venice itself, and the enormous sum of six hundred thousand ducats by the noble court of the Quarantia. Accompanied to his new *palazzo* by a triumphant

Facing:
Giovanni Battista Tiepolo's fresco celebrating the *Apotheosis of Admiral Vettor Pisani* was commissioned by Chiara Pisani in 1746. Traditionally, the work was identified as *Mars and Venus*.

procession of noble gondolas and laurel-bedecked boats, the "glorious youth," as one local chronicler of the day called him, was now ready to play his new role as a man of substance. Nevertheless, litigation continued and was exacerbated by Pietro's marriage to the noblewoman, Laura Zusto, in 1785. The *nobil uomo* died in 1847, having like many other Venetian aristocrats been made a count of the Austro-Hungarian empire, whereupon he took the predicate Bagnolo. He left as heir his son Vettor Daniele, the last of the Pisanis of San Polo, whose line became

extinct with his three daughters. In the living room overlooking the Grand Canal, which opens to the right of the *pòrtego*, Giambattista Tiepolo spent the summer of 1743 frescoing the ceiling with a superb *Apotheosis of Admiral Vettor Pisani*. A complex, light-filled artistic achievement, it is typical of Tiepolo's classical period, which began three years earlier in Milan when he was commissioned to decorate Palazzo Clerici.

The baroque trompe l'oeil effects framing the fresco are the work of Francesco Zanchi. The subject of the

painting is the glorification of the most illustrious ancestor of Tiepolo's patron, Chiara Pisani. Vettor Pisani was a *capitano da mar*, an admiral victorious in 1380 in the war of Chioggia over Venice's sworn enemies, the Genoese. As an ancestor, he was more mythical than real, for Vettor belonged to a different family of Pisanis that became extinct in the early eighteenth century. Instead of the proud Moretta Pisani lion, Vettor's family emblem was the wily weasel. The painting has, in fact, only recently been identified as his *Apotheosis*; traditionally, it was interpreted as *Mars and Venus*. This masterly work is dominated by the triumphant carriage of Vettor, the family hero and guardian spirit of the house of Pisani. The room, with its rocaille furnishings and red brocade-covered walls, also housed the pride of the Pisani art collection, the *Family of Darius at the Feet of Alexander*, painted in the latter half of the sixteenth century by Paolo Veronese and today substituted by a fine old copy. The original was sold in 1857 and is in the National Gallery in London. Commissioned by the indefatigable Chiara Pisani two hundred years after the original as a companion piece for the Veronese work, *The Death of Darius* by Giovan Battista Piazzetta, painted in 1746, once hung on the opposite wall. Today, it is on display at Ca' Rezzonico in Venice. The Correr Museum is now the home of another masterpiece that once hung in Palazzo Pisani Moretta, *Dedalus and Icarus*, the sculpture that the young Antonio Canova created in 1778 and 1779 for the *procuratore*, Pietro Vettor Pisani "da San Polo." The finest works in the art collection at Palazzo Pisani Moretta were removed from its halls during the nineteenth century, after the demise of the Most Serene Republic.

Nevertheless, the residence is still one of Venice's most complete and best preserved, both for its magnificent paintings and stuccoes, which bear witness to rocaille's final moments of glory and the emergence of neoclassicism, and for the impressive array of eighteenth-century furniture and *objets d'art*. These include armchairs, elaborate mirrors, consoles, ceramics, and porcelain from the local Vezzi and Cozzi factories, precious fabrics, glassware, and so on, down to sophisticated details like the gilt vegetal curtain rail of the *Salone Giallo*, or Yellow Room, which sets the scene for a metamorphic natural masquerade in an exquisitely eighteenth-century taste.

PALAZZO BARBARO
VENICE, VENETO

After several decades in painful obscurity, by the end of the nineteenth century the Most Serene Republic had regained a brighter, more cosmopolitan atmosphere. It was the perfect setting for a sophisticated society of European aristocrats and intellectuals, flamboyant Russian grand dukes, and eccentric expatriate Britons, while the United States contributed a miscellany of cynical tycoons, naive or mischievous heiresses in search of a title to marry, snobs, elegant gentlemen of leisure, and earnest enthusiasts of literature and the arts. In 1885, the *palazzo* was acquired by a Bostonian couple, the Curtises, from Dottor Cesare Musatti, the *nobildonna* Matilde Barbaro having sold off her family property in the middle of the century. The nineteenth century began just after the final collapse of the Venetian republic in 1797. Over the course of the following decades, this noble residence looking onto the Grand Canal at San Vidal itself went into decline, and was even stripped of the paintings with which Giambattista

Tiepolo had decorated the rooms in the mid-eighteenth century. The Curtises, who came from the cream of Boston society, had left their native shores for personal reasons. When they arrived in the lagoon, they first rented Palazzo Barbaro, later deciding to purchase, for the sum of 70,000 francs, the equivalent of 13,500 dollars at the time, the second *piano nobile* story of the building and the third floor, with its elegant library. They did not acquire the mezzanine, owned by Countess Pisani. In a letter, Ariana Curtis stressed that the residence was worth much more, if only for the superb eighteenth-century decor, adding that to renovate the sunflowers and mother-of-pearl dining room floor would have cost as much as 15,000 francs!

There then began an extensive campaign of restoration, both on the fabric of the *palazzo* and on its decoration. The stuccoes in the ballroom were consolidated, the Gothic arch of the entrance on the Grand Canal was recovered, and the master smith Bellotto was commissioned to provide new historicist grills modeled on the gate of the Norman abbey of Fécamp. Again in the ballroom, the paintings on the ceiling were cleaned of the bitumen with which they had been coated by a previous tenant. The central canvas was revealed to the thrilled Curtises in its original beauty as a *Roman Triumph, with Zenobia before the Victor, Her Hands Bound with Strings of Pearls.* The courtyard was provided with a well curb using a capital, perhaps "from San Marco or the Doge's Palace," which was acquired from the workshop of Biondetti, the stonemason in San Vio. The Curtises' home became a focus of social and intellectual life in late nineteenth- and early twentieth-century Venice, a decadent, languid muse that inspired Wagner, d'Annunzio, de Musset, and Proust.

The celebrated American novelist Henry James spent much time in Venice. From 1887, he lodged mainly with his fellow Bostonians, the Curtises, drawing on these experiences for his novels *The Wings of the Dove* and *The Aspern Papers.* However, James was not the only celebrity of the day to frequent the *palazzo*'s sophisticated reception rooms. Isabella Stewart Gardner was a rich, rapacious collector not only of Renaissance paintings, but also of ancient stone artifacts, such as the loggia from the neighboring Palazzo Cavalli-Franchetti, which she acquired while Boito was restoring it. Today, it is in the Venetian Court of the museum in Boston that bears her name. At Palazzo Barbaro, Stewart Gardner found architectural and artistic inspiration, establishing important connections with European society. John Singer Sargent arrived in 1899, when he painted the entire Curtis family in the *salone.* This famous multiple portrait hangs today in the Royal Academy in London. Other visitors included Claude Monet and assorted members of Europe's royal families, including the empress of Prussia, daughter of Queen Victoria of the United Kingdom, and Princess Louise of Sweden. The nineteenth century may have been an extraordinary period of renewal for Palazzo Barbaro, but we should not forget its previous history, or its role as the home of one of Venice's most prominent aristocratic families.

The present complex comprises two buildings that have been joined together. The earlier building is Gothic and has airy fifteenth-century lines, enhanced by the classical notes of its polychrome marble disks and heads of Roman emperors, tangible proof of the humanist taste cultivated with such tenacious enthusiasm by the San Vidal Barbaros. This branch of the family produced many eminent men of letters, including the Francesco Barbaro who chose the commemorative inscription on the bronze monument to Gattamelata, the Umbrian *condottiero,* or mercenary captain, in the pay of the Venetians, which stands on the parvis of the Basilica of Sant'Antonio in Padua. Although the family produced no doges, the Barbaros traced their roots to Pola and Aquileia, and dated their arrival in the lagoon to A.D. 868. They were always respected as one of the most influential families of the

Venetian aristocracy after the *serrata*, or closure, of the Maggior Consiglio, which in 1297 concentrated public power in the hands of the longest-established houses of the native aristocracy. Ermolao (Almorò in Venetian) Barbaro was the son of the *procuratore* (magistrate) and *cavaliere* (knight) Zaccaria Barbaro, *provveditore in campo* (civilian army commander) against the Estense armies, who in 1465 acquired the *palazzo* from Lucia Coppo, a widow whose married name was Aldioni. Ermolao's mother was Chiara Vendramin, daughter of the doge, learned humanist and scholar, Andrea Vendramin, a diplomat and *bailo*, or Venetian resident at Constantinople.

Ermolao was disgraced and died in exile in 1493 for having been constrained two years earlier to accept a cardinalate and the prestigious nomination to the patriarchate of Aquileia by Innocent VIII, before he had been able to obtain permission from the Venetian republic. Another Barbaro patriarch of Aquileia was Daniele, who died in 1570. A cultivated priest, Daniele was also an ambassador, influential politician, and patron, with his brother Marc'Antonio, of Palladio, who built for them the stupendous Barbaro villa at Maser. Antonio Barbaro, *provveditore generale* (governor) in Dalmatia and from 1675 to 1678 the republic's diplomatic representative at the Roman court of Innocent XI, left on his death in 1678 a bequest of 30,000 ducats for the construction of the facade of the church of Santa Maria del Giglio in Venice, to plans by Giuseppe Sardi. It is a triumph of baroque art, raised to the greater glory of a private family, and was the object of much contemporary controversy. The figures of five Barbaros who distinguished themselves on the field of battle stand in the places usually reserved for statues of

Facing above and below:
Detail from one of the imposing canvases that grace the ballroom. The subject is the *Rape of the Sabines* and the work was painted by Sebastiano Ricci, probably around 1699.

The stuccoed and frescoed eighteenth-century library on the second floor of the *palazzo*. Its austere bookcases contain hundreds of ancient codices and printed books.

Below:
The ballroom was designed by Antonio Gaspari, one of late seventeenth-century Venice's most flamboyant architects. The stucco decoration provides a fitting setting for the marvelous paintings by Giovanni Battista Piazzetta and Sebastiano Ricci.

saints. In the middle, the allegorical statues of Virtue and Honor in the upper order flank the dominant figure of Antonio Barbaro, portrayed by Juste Le Court.

Let us return to Palazzo Barbaro itself, before it came into the possession of the family, when it was purchased from the relict of Nicolò Aldioni. Previously, the property had belonged to an apothecary, Pietro Franco, and even earlier, to a prominent family of "original citizens," the Spieras. We know that, in 1425, the *palazzo* was under construction and that the *tajapiera*, or stonemason, Giovanni Bon was working on it. Bon belonged to a noted family of stonemasons who were also busy at the Doge's Palace and Marin Contarini's Ca' d'Oro.

The second part of the Palazzo Barbaro building was the result of restructuring carried out for Alvise Barbaro from 1694 to 1698 by architect Antonio Gaspari, one of Venice's finest, best informed, and freest interpreters of Baroque. Gaspari added a ballroom and to house it, he rebuilt in the contemporary idiom an edifice that stood adjacent to the Gothic wing. His late seventeenth-century contribution has lent an especially splendid atmosphere to the interior. The *pòrtego* in the fifteenth-century part of the house is further adorned with paintings by Bambini and Segala, set in appropriate frames, at the instruction of Alvise Barbaro and his consort, Marina Grimani. An inventory from 1699 reveals that the ceiling of the *cameron* (the main reception room) was already graced with five canvasses by Antonio Zanchi. Complemented on the walls by *cuori d'oro* — the leather panels decorated with gold leaf for which Cordoba in Spain was famous during the Renaissance — the paintings represent episodes of female virtue in line with Roman ideals of heroism.

The paintings on the ceiling are dedicated to the classical queens, Artemisia and Zenobia, the Sabine Ersilia, wife of Romulus, Hypsicratea, the concubine of Mithridates, and to the Roman heroine, Clelia. These were complemented by two large-scale wall paintings, *The Rape of the Sabines* by Sebastiano Ricci, dated 1698, and *Coriolanus Supplicated by the Women of Rome to End the War against the Sabines*, by Antonio Balestra, which probably dates from 1709. These were followed later, perhaps as late as 1744, by Giambattista Piazzetta's *Mucius Scaevola*. The iconography uses episodes from the

early history of Rome to trace an allegorical scheme that alludes to Venice as the "third Rome." This was a constant sixteenth-century leitmotiv at Venice, which had taken up the political heritage and transfigured the imagery of the ancient city of the Caesars. This series of paintings is a mid eighteenth-century echo of the original oligarchic pride of the republic, expressed in the motto *non nobis, Domine, sed Urbis genio* (Not for Us, Lord, but for the Spirit of the City) that announced on the fronts of the patrician houses the first stirrings of the Venetian Renaissance, almost in apology for the magnificence of their setting. This highly symbolic, classically-inspired scene was also adopted at Palazzo Barbaro, the seat of a noble house that had long been familiar with the papal court. In contrast to the rigid, protectionist orthodoxy practiced by the hard core of Venice's oligarchy, the Barbaros were very receptive of the new intellectual movements. Alvise's son, Almorò, married three times to ensure the family an heir. His first consort, Modesta Valier was followed by Andriana Contarini and, finally in 1736, Cecilia Emo. Almorò at last united the section of the *palazzo* owned by his mother, who died in 1733, to the rest of the building, then began a sumptuous program of redecoration, in preparation for his probable election to the high post of *procuratore di San Marco* (he was in fact nominated in 1750).

The *salone* was given the full baroque treatment, which left it replete with gold and white stucco, embellished with *putti,* floral designs, reliefs, elaborate frames, shells, and double-headed eagles charged on the breast "with a crescent argent, an *annulet gules.*" The stucco frames the paintings on the ceiling, then descends spectacularly to invade the walls, brushing aside the more old-fashioned "gold hearts" (*cuori d'oro),* and providing a single backdrop for the three great works by Ricci, Balestra, and Piazzetta. Giambattista Tiepolo's works complied with this sequential logic, and were themed to exalt female virtues through figures from antiquity. The motif proceeds in a series of significant episodes, from *Latinus Offering his*

Daughter Lavinia in Marriage to Aeneas, today in the museum at Copenhagen, to *Tarquinius and Lucretia,* now at the Staatsgalerie in Hamburg, and the unidentified scene from classical history in the National Gallery of Art in Washington, to the painting now at the High Museum in Atlanta depicting *Roman Matrons Making Offerings to Juno.*

The paintings by Tiepolo, which are the latest chronologically in the overall scheme, have pre-ordained spaces in the stucco grid, which must therefore have been completed around 1750, when the artist was working on his contribution. The stuccoes reveal many similarities to the extravagant ceiling of soaring *putti* at Palazzo Albrizzi in Sant'Aponal. Two of the leading names in eighteenth-century stucco at Venice have been put forward as its possible authors, Abbondio Stazio and Carpoforo Mazzetti, known as *Tencalla.* These two Lugano artists worked successfully together on Venice's most fashionable interiors, combining the dying moments of baroque with the nascent rocaille idiom. However, they cannot be the real creators as Stazio died in August 1745 and all trace of *Tencalla* is lost after December of the same year. Almorò Barbaro also turned his attention to the remodeling of a *tinello,* the dining room in the north wing of the third floor of the Gothic building, which was renovated between 1745 and 1750.

The terrazzo, or Venetian mosaic, floor is of the type known as *arlecchino* (harlequin) from the wide range of colors in its stone tesserae. Here, the effect is further enhanced by iridescent mother-of-pearl inserts scattered throughout the floral design. The original ceiling painting was removed in 1874 and is exhibited at the Metropolitan Museum of Art in New York (a copy is now in its place). In 1752, Giambattista Tiepolo was commissioned to paint the vault over the great staircase in the palace built by Balthasar Neumann for the prelates of the Schönborn family. Here, the ceiling painting was yet another of Tiepolo's imaginative, nostalgic visions aimed at showering glory on the fading Ancien Régime in a solemn, anachronistic death-dream of baroque absolutism.

Another remarkable feature of the *palazzo* is the fourth floor library, a quiet, refined ambience where the ceiling stuccoes are less intrusive, showing a lighter, rocaille touch. It is especially reminiscent of Henry James, who lived and worked here. This noble residence, already split up into several properties, is currently being divided further.

THE DOGE'S PALACE
VENICE, VENETO

Facing:
On the ground floor of the wing of the Palace that looks onto the *Ponte della Paglia* bridge is a scene from the *Stories of Noah*. At the same corner, on the floor above, is a fourteenth-century Archangel Raphael next to Tobit.

Following pages:
The architecture of the Doge's Palace underwent many alterations over the centuries as Venice's political status evolved, first from duchy to commune, then to Most Serene Seigneury, and finally to the Most Serene Republic.

The home of government, the residence of the doge, and the seat of the highest magistracies of the Most Serene Republic (a court, state archive, armory, and prison), this enormous building was for several centuries the setting for the most significant episodes in the history of Venice. *Palazzo Ducale* (the Doge's Palace) was the only building in the city permitted to be called a *palazzo*, distinguishing it from all the noble residences, which are called *ca'*, a short form of *casa*, or house, but also of *casada*, which means family.

The Gothic grace of the Doge's Palace proudly yet elegantly dominates the waters of the Bacino di San Marco and faces onto Venice's only true square, Piazza San Marco, or Saint Mark's Square. The *piazza*, too, is endowed with its own symbolic uniqueness. All the other public spaces carved out of the network of canals and close-packed buildings are known by the lesser names *campo* and *campiello*. The Doge's Palace witnessed moments of tragedy and glory, the enduring magnificence and sumptuous decline of the Venetian republic, its intrigues, conspiracies, defeats, victories, executions, triumphs, feasts, and opulently emblematic rituals. It was here that in 1797, the final session of the Maggior Consiglio, or Grand Council, voted to declare the end of the republic, deposing the last doge, the Friulian Ludovico Manin, and leaving the field free for the revolutionary armies of Napoleon Bonaparte. Only a handful of the most determined nobles in that huge assembly were resolved to resist to the death, and perish like the heroes of classical times on the ashes of their homeland.

The Doge's Palace was built in three distinct stages and styles, Byzantine, Gothic, and Renaissance, the latter two fusing to produce the superb architectural

Above:
The balcony completed by Antonio Abbondi and Sansovino in 1536 features a statue of the doge Andrea Gritti at the feet of the lion of Saint Mark, the work of the sixteenth-century sculptors, Danese Cattaneo and Pietro da Salò.

Left:
The porphyry group of Tetrarchs embracing under the Torre del Tesoro may have belonged to the ancient ducal castle erected in A.D. 810.

jewel that has survived to our day. The complex houses works of art created to glorify Venice's political and economic power. Formerly turreted, and perhaps built on the foundations of a classical fortification, the Doge's Palace began its long career in A.D. 810, when Agnello Parteciaco, fleeing from the Frankish invaders, transferred the capital of the duchy of Venice from Malamocco to the better protected Realtine islands. From the start, the building was closely linked to the doge himself, as the original role as a monarch was transformed into the first magistrate of the Venetian state.

Eventually, the Doge's Palace assumed the spectacular, albeit intangible, role of emblem and symbolic container of a parliamentary power. As medieval Venice gradually asserted its authority, magistratures and offices multiplied. There

Facing:
The *Scala dei Giganti*, at the top of which newly elected doges were crowned, owes its name to the statues of *Mars and Neptune* by Jacopo Sansovino, which were added in 1566.

Left:
At the *Porta della Carta*, the doge Francesco Foscari kneels before a lion.

Below:
The bell tower, church facade, and abbey of San Giorgio Maggiore seen from the *Loggia Foscara* at the Doge's Palace.

was a need for suitable accommodation that proclaimed to the world the majesty of Venice, Queen of the Mediterranean and, after the fall of Constantinople in 1453, the Third Rome. Venice passed from being a duchy, to a commune, then a Most Serene Seigneury, and finally a Most Serene Republic. The doge's function as a mere representative of the republic is clear from the ducal apartments, a modest area in comparison with the spaces given over to constitutional organs, especially the huge, lavishly decorated hall of the *Maggior Consiglio,* dominated by Jacopo Tintoretto's immense sixteenth-century canvas of *Paradise.* The *Maggior Consiglio* was the "Lord of the Republic." Comprising every male member of the aristocracy over the age of twenty-five, it

was the fountainhead of all elective power. The executive and much of the legislative power lay with the Senate, presided by the Pien Collegio. The Senate had meeting rooms and anterooms, such as the *Sala delle Quattro Porte* (Room of the Four Doors), constructed in 1575 by Antonio da Ponte and decorated with allegorical paintings by Titian, then two centuries later by Giambattista Tiepolo, and the *Salotto Quadrato* (Square Room), equally resplendent with gilt wooden coffered ceilings, superb paintings, and other decorations.

The celebrated *Consiglio dei Dieci,* or Council of Ten, was a legislative, executive, and judicial organ. Its home was a series of rooms adjacent to the armories, munitions stores, and prisons.

These last included the *Piombi*, the awful, lead-covered cells under the roof (freezing cold in winter and burning hot in summer) from which the eighteenth-century adventurer Giacomo Casanova made a daring escape. Other places of incarceration were the *Torresella* and the *Pozzi*, or wells, on the first floor, which were often under water at high tide. The *Ponte dei Sospiri*, or Bridge of Sighs, leads to the more recent Palazzo delle Prigioni, separated from the massive bulk of the Doge's Palace by a canal. There was also an executive arm that implemented the decisions of the Ten, the three Capi, the three Inquisitors of State, the three *Avogadori di Comun*, or state lawyers, who guaranteed the constitutionality of proceedings, and the judicial magistracies, such as the *Quarantie* and the *Piovego*, the magistrates with responsibility for the water supply and problems concerning the lagoon.

The *palazzo* we see today took shape from the fourteenth to the sixteenth century and can rightly be regarded as the community's collective royal palace, the very symbol of the Most Serene Republic. Its structure is the result of a collective expression of will, not that of a

single ruler. Many doges succeeded each other before the fateful year of 1797, when Venice's independent existence was extinguished forever. Some were impressive figures, like Andrea Gritti or Sebastiano Venier, others were pale or ephemeral, while yet others attempted to transform the republic's institutions into a hereditary monarchy. Every doge would bring his own furniture, paintings,

household objects, and ornaments to furnish the rooms in the *palazzo* reserved for him. Decisions to restructure the fabric and decoration of the building were always taken collectively, although they bear the name of a single doge. This was the case in 1340, after the *serrata*, or closure, of the *Maggior Consiglio* in 1297, when the growing number of council members made the building of a larger

and lovelier hall imperative. It also happened after the many terrible fires, such as the ones in 1483 or 1574, or the disastrous conflagration of 1577. After 1297, the nobles ran the republic of Saint Mark through their assembly for half a millennium.

In the fourteenth century, when the great construction facing onto the *piazzetta* and the quay was being built,

we find Pietro Baseggio and a certain Enrico. Scholars have abandoned the traditional identification of the architect with the *tagiapiera*, or mason, Filippo Calendario, who was hanged as an accomplice in the conspiracy of the doge Marin Faliero in 1355. The Gothic facade of the Doge's Palace set an architectural precedent that for long was identified with the very image of the Most Serene Republic itself. The polyphonic symphony of the three-lobed, pointed-arch, second-floor galleries, the *biblia pauperum*, or pauper's Bible, of fourteenth-century carvings that adorn the capitals, and those on the building's corners, excited the admiring comments of John Ruskin in the nineteenth century, as he reports in *The Stones of Venice*. In the humanist fifteenth century, we find the name of the Verona architect and sculptor, Antonio Rizzo. We also note Pietro Solari, *Il Lombardo*, Giorgio Spavento, and Antonio Abbondi, known as *Lo Scarpagnino*, all striving for a formula that would bridge the gap separating a Venice tenaciously clinging to its own Gothic imagery and the new artistic and architectural movements arriving from central Italy.

Venice reacted by hiding behind her gilded curtain of Gothic art, seeking Renaissance solutions that would blend with the local tradition, such as the *colorismo* of the Lombardo family, which recovered the Venetian-Byzantine idiom and the cultured approach of Mauro Codussi. However, it was Jacopo Sansovino, arriving in the lagoon from the splendors of papal Rome just before the sack of the Eternal City by imperial troops in 1527, who finally opened Venice to the Renaissance. Sansovino created the superb *Scala d'Oro*, its vault studded with the late sixteenth-century stuccoes of Alessandro Vittoria. Here, too, as in the nearby great staircase of the Libreria Marciana, allegorical frescoes by Battista Franco framed in obviously Mannerist scrolls have been inserted between the robustly ribbed sail vaults. During the course of the sixteenth century, the various *proti*, or works supervisors, were orthodox interpreters of the political programs of the republic's nobility. Two such were Bartolomeo Manopola and Antonio Da Ponte, who was preferred to the classical vision of Andrea Palladio. Nevertheless, Palladio, too, was summoned to labor on the never-ending building project that was the Doge's Palace, in the Senate's rooms and its appendages, and for the rebuilding of the Rialto bridge, destroyed by fire in 1514.

A legion of artists was employed

Facing:
The *Scala d'Oro* was begun after 1554 by Sansovino and finished in 1558 by Scarpagnino. This breathtaking staircase owes its name to the gilt stuccoes by Alessandro Vittorio. The paintings in the vault are by Battista Franco.

Right:
The *Sala delle Quattro Porte*, where Veronese's *Rape of Europa* hangs, is also the home of Titian's *The Doge Antonio Grimani Kneeling Before the Faith*. The room was designed by Palladio and Giovanni Antonio Rusconi then built in 1575 by Antonio da Ponte.

Below:
The *Sala dell'Anticollegio* with two canvases by Tintoretto. On the left are Mercury and the three Graces while *Minerva Sending away Mars from Peace and Prosperity* hangs on the other side of the door.

Above:
The *Sala del Senato* was also known as the *Sala dei Pregadi* (Room of the Invited). Here, the sixty senators were "invited" to meet with the magistrates who held various offices.

Facing:
The *Sala del Collegio* and Veronese's allegorical painting in celebration of Doge Sebastiano Venier and his victory at Lepanto.

Following pages:
The vast *Paradise* painted by Tintoretto and his assistants between 1588 and 1592 in the *Sala del Maggior Consiglio.*

for centuries on an endless building project of boundless magnificence. There were sculptors like the Gothic Bon family, the Dalle Masegnes and Matteo Raverti, in the fifteenth and sixteenth centuries Pietro and Tullio Lombardo, at the height of the sixteenth century the great Sansovino, followed by Alessandro Vittoria, Tiziano Aspetti from Padua, and the Florentines Rosso and Lamberti who decorated the capitals of the pillars supporting the two

colossal, polychrome fourteenth-century facades. We find the Padua-born master of Gothic art, Guariento, the sophisticated Pisanello of the Este and Gonzaga courts, then the chivalrous Gentile da Fabriano, through to the Vivarinis and Bellinis, who took Venice from the elaborate decoration of the Gothic period to the new achievements of the Renaissance. Here, too, we see the brother-in-law of Andrea Mantegna, the sublime Giovanni Bellini,

Dedicated to the patron saint chosen by the Venetians to replace the Byzantine Saint Theodore, Saint Mark's was erected four years after the saint's body had been removed from Alexandria. The new place of worship was invested with even more civic than religious significance, declaring to the world Venice's withdrawal from the Eastern Roman Empire and its own political supremacy. The basilica's long history is interwoven with that of the neighboring Doge's Palace, as may be seen from the view paintings of eighteenth-century artists like Marieschi, Canaletto, and Bellotto to the early Romantic melancholy of Francesco Guardi, whose Saint Mark's Square is crowded with the red robes of bewigged magistrates and ladies sporting masks. On the waters of the Bacino opposite, gondolas mingle with gilded eight-oared *bissone* and the great forty-oared ducal *bucintoro* in never-ending, self-referential celebration of the declining republic.

in whose workshop Tiziano Vecellio, Titian, learned his art. Then there came a hiatus, an enforced interruption occasioned by the frequent fires that broke out in the late fifteenth and sixteenth centuries. The next stars were Titian, who endlessly renewed his art over the long decades of his distinguished career, and the generation of Mannerists inspired by the arrival in the lagoon from Florence, in 1546, of Giorgio Vasari. The roll call includes Paolo Veronese, Jacopo Tintoretto, then the Bassanos, Verona-born Bonifazio de' Pitati, the elegant, tormented Tuscan artist, Francesco Salviati, Antonio Vassillacchi, known as *L'Aliense*, the Vicenza artist, Giambattista Zelotti, and Jacopo Palma Giovane, in the seventeenth century, Pietro Liberi, down to the dazzling art of the eighteenth-century master, Giambattista Tiepolo. The neighboring basilica of Saint Mark's served as both the doge's chapel and as a church of state. Saint Mark's itself is modeled on the greatest of the imperial basilicas at Constantinople, Hagia Sophia (Church of the Holy Wisdom) and Hagioi Apostoloi (Holy Apostles).

VILLA BARBARO
"VILLA MASER"
MASER, VENETO

residential building. This stands on the same level as its functional appendages and reveals its special status as a home in the audaciously disproportionate, mannerist-inspired pediment, which is split in its entablature and dominates the sober facade with its nimble Ionic engaged columns. A spectacular stucco relief bears the Barbaro family coat of arms (argent, a double-headed eagle displayed sable crowned or charged on the breast with a crescent argent, an

Villa Barbaro at Maser stands on a gentle slope at the foot of the hills that roll across the Veneto flatlands to the Alps in the north. The villa is an example of Palladio's more advanced conception of the elegant country residence. Here, the architect has introduced elements characteristic of the region's farmyards in the dovecots and *barchessa* outbuildings. The former are set in elegant pavilions at either end of the construction, masked by facades bearing sundials surmounted by tympanum panels and flanked by upturned-arch side elements, whereas the *barchesse* form harmonious porticos attached to the sides of the main

Above:
This portrait by Paolo Veronese is a likeness of Daniele Barbaro, patriarch of Aquileia who in 1566 translated and wrote a commentary on Vitruvius' *De Re Architectura*.

Right:
A general view of the main facade of Villa Barbaro. The residence is in line with the *barchesse*, ancillary constructions that were customarily used for farming purposes.

annulet gules) amidst naked classical figures, *putti*, spiral motifs, garlands, and bucranes. It is projected by the impact of the central balcony on the entablature above, its sophisticatedly theatrical emphasis inspired by the decorative repertoire adopted in France at the Château of Fontainebleau in the third and fourth decade of the sixteenth century by Rosso Fiorentino and Primaticcio.

The concept underlying the Maser complex clearly stands apart from the mainstream of Palladian villas. It is not intended to be a point of focus for the farmland for it is not located on the flat. Instead, it stands on the edge of the fields, on a slight slope. As we have seen, it does not comply with the usual hierarchy of buildings, based on individual functions. At Maser, the owner's residence continues into the *barchesse*, which are normally used for agricultural purposes. The dovecot towers seem to vie with the projecting volume of

Above:
The colors of springtime contrast the whiteness of this statue of a divinity against the pale green of the first leaves and the sapphire blue of a gathering storm.

the two-story main building in the middle of the group. There is no *pronaos* with free columns. Instead, the central section flaunts four Ionic columns bearing a dramatic tympanum panel. The configuration of the horizontal plan is, in some respects, reminiscent of Villa Emo at Fanzolo.

The principals who commissioned this architectural invention could only have been themselves exceptional and particularly *au courant*. Above all, they must have taken an active part in the overall design of their country residence, and in drafting the artistic and allegorical programs for the decoration of the interior. Daniele Barbaro was the ambassador of the Most Serene Republic to England, and then patriarch of Aquileia. He was also the translator and commentator of Vitruvius' *De Re Architectura*, published in 1556, and for which he had asked Palladio to provide the illustrations. His brother, Marcantonio, was born in 1518 and died in 1595. An

113

outstandingly able diplomat at the courts of London and Constantinople, Daniele had been permitted by Henry VIII to include the Tudor rose in his own coat of arms. He was also a senator, a *provveditore generale in Terraferma* (magistrate in charge of Venice's mainland territories), *procuratore di sopra* (one of the nine *procuratori di San Marco* magistrates), *provveditore al Sale* (magistrate in charge of salt), *provveditore all'Arsenale* (magistrate in charge of shipyards), reformer of the university of Padua, and an amateur sculptor. Both brothers could fairly be described as leading figures in mid sixteenth-century Venice. The Barbaros were one of the most illustrious, and wealthiest, noble families in the city. The ecclesiastic, Daniele, a sophisticated humanist with close links to the papal court, was involved with the Accademia della Fama, while Marcantonio, one of the three *provveditori* entrusted with the rebuilding

of the Rialto bridge, had lobbied in vain in favor of Palladio's flamboyant "Romanizing" design. In his capacity as *savio all'eresia* (magistrate with jurisdiction in religious matters), Barbaro was, however, able to protect the brilliant artist Paolo Veronese when he was accused of irreverence for having depicted an over-sumptuous *Last Supper* for the friars of Santi Giovanni e Paolo. Barbaro's simple but shrewd solution was to change the work's title to *Feast in the House of Levi*.

Palladio's plans for Maser were drafted at the end of the fifth decade of the sixteenth century. The villa was to be erected on land that the Barbaro family had owned since 1339, and was conceived as the country residence of the *nobil homo* Marcantonio, his wife Giustiniana Giustiniani, and their four children. The Barbaros wanted a "Roman" villa, based on Pliny's description of the Villa Laurentina and contemporary constructions in Rome. One supremely Roman element is the *nymphaeum*, the *pièce de résistance* of the country residences of nobles and cardinals. We need only mention the most famous of these, the nymphaeum at Villa Giulia. A small, rectangular *hortus conclusus*, or enclosed garden, is tucked away at the back of the residence. In the middle is a semi-elliptical pool, leading to a circular grotto. Here stands a river god, pouring forth water from the spring behind and distributing it to the ornamental fountains and fishponds. The water then emerged from the villa's Edenic seclusion to irrigate

orchards, kitchen gardens, vineyards, and farmland.

Water, the symbolic, alchemic giver of life was at the heart of every mannerist garden. With the exception of a few minor details that may have been the work of Marcantonio Barbaro himself, the generously distributed stucco decorations and sculptures are the impressive contribution of Alessandro Vittoria, follower and collaborator of Sansovino, born in Trento in 1525. The figure of a river god, a frequent topos of the Roman garden, after the model of the Belvedere court in the Vatican, had never before been adopted in the Veneto. There were, however, further borrowings from Rome

by these refined patrons. The insistence on imagery taken from the Eternal City was, for the Barbaros, a precise political statement of the good standing they enjoyed at the papal court. The link was reinforced by Daniele Barbaro's ancient and prestigious title of patriarch of Aquileia, older even than the corresponding rank at Venice. Another clearly Roman element is the small circular-plan temple on the road to the southeast, erected to a design by Palladio in 1580, ten years after Daniele's death. It is a pantheon in miniature, displaying the same cubic volume and similar architectural elements, such as the *pronaos*, the stepped dome, and the apses that alternate inside with *edicules* that house Alessandro Vittoria's stucco sculptures. The French theme is also evident in the influence of the sixteenth-century chapel at Château d'Anet by Philibert de l'Orme.

Facing:
A lovely view of the *Stanza di Bacco*, or Bacchus room, with its impressive fireplace created by Alessandro Vittoria. It bears a celebrated Latin invitation to serenity, *Ignem In Sinu Ne Abscondas* (Harbor No Malice in Thy Breast).

Left:
In the *Stanza dell'Olimpo*, life-size frescoed figures look down on the room below. The noble lady of the house, Giustiniana Giustinian, holds two roses in her right hand as she smiles a greeting to her guests.

Below:
The ceiling of the *Stanza dell'Olimpo*, or Olympus Room. In the center of the vault, a dazzling *Wisdom* is surrounded by the gods of the planets with the signs of the Zodiac. The lunette frames the figures of *Summer* and *Autumn*.

Let us return to the villa, which was restored at great expense in the 1930s by Tomaso Buzzi for Count Giuseppe Volpi di Misurata, whose descendants still own it. Many artists of the period joined forces with Volpi and contributed to this sophisticated restoration campaign, whose impact is still evident in the villa's conceptual elegance, both in the private rooms and in the part open to the public. There is an undisputed masterpiece in the fresco cycle completed by Paolo Veronese between 1561 and 1563 for the walls of the rooms on the *piano nobile*. Veronese was assisted by his brother, Benedetto, and various other collaborators. This magisterial work establishes a spatial hierarchy in the building based on the bilateral symmetry dominated by the cross-plan entrance hall and completed by the northern extremity. In this way, the *salone*, too, generates its own hierarchy of images. Palladio and Veronese collaborated closely at Maser to implement a superb joint project. In compliance with the dicta of Vitruvius, the painted decorations are an integral part of the concept and architecture of the villa. The paintings occupied entire walls, framed by fluted Corinthian columns raised on imitation marble bases, and set against an illusionistic landscape. We are regaled with arches, architraves, trompe l'oeil decorations, Arcadian perspectives that take on the appearance of reality, Olympic deities, vigorous nudes, *putti*, servants, and everyday figures painted full size in the dress of the day so that they seem to be walking, tangible yet metaphysical presences, into or out of the paintings.

The members of the Barbaro family eternally observe nature and her rhythms from a painted balcony in the main reception room and, at the end of the corridor, a nobleman dressed for the hunt is entering through an illusionistic door, accompanied by his retriever. The iconographic scheme must have been inspired by the vast learning of the patrons, especially Daniele, one of the most erudite humanists of the day. The dominant theme is harmony, especially family harmony, and the fusion of classical mythology with Christian doctrine in a single concept of nature. Governed by the Muses and the planets of the empyrean, and guided by

118

meditations on immortality, life at the noble house unfolded happily in the shelter of its rural station, represented by the landscapes on the lower walls of the *piano nobile*. The views lead the eye along the constant line of the horizon to the arch window with balcony that opens onto the Barbaro estates. These were themes that Bembo had already elaborated in his circle at Asolo in the early sixteenth century. All this is presented in rooms with exciting names, such as the Olympus Room, the Dog Room, the Lantern Room, the Cross Room, the Bacchus Room, and the Court of Love Room. Veronese's pictorial repertoires at Maser, immediately imitated and popularized by the artist's successors, such as Zelotti at Villa Emo, Fanzolo, exercised enormous influence for two centuries on generations of artists, inspiring major creative geniuses and lesser painters. Above all, Veronese influenced the eighteenth-century master Giambattista Tiepolo, who admired his magnificent, pioneering work at Villa Barbaro in the mid-sixteenth century.

Facing:
The *Stanza del Tribunale d'Amore.* On the vaulted ceiling of the Court of Love Room, the bride sits facing the judge, who is flanked by the allegorical figures of Truth and Justice. It is clear that the story will have a happy ending from the *putti* flitting joyfully overhead, showering her with flowers.

Facing lower left:
The massive feigned Corinthian columns in the *Stanza dell'Olimpo* frame mountains and rivers that hark back to the peace and serenity of a lost Arcadian past.

Right:
Detail of one of the many fresco decorations in the *Crociera.* This riverscape dotted with ruins is peopled by country folk moving in a fairy-tale atmosphere where time stands still and the wan colors are barely hinted at. Classical reminiscences and fragments of rural life, which might have come from the contemporary farces of Ruzante, mingle with an easy insouciance.

Villa Almerico Capra Valmarana "La Rotonda"
Vicenza, Veneto

Above:
Andrea Palladio conceived La Rotonda as a monument to his patron, Vincenza-born Paolo Almerico, apostolic referendary to Pius IV and Pius V.

Facing:
His architectural solution hinges on an Ionic *pronaos*, which is replicated on all four sides of the villa.

"The site is one of the most delightful and pleasant it is possible to find. For it stands on an easily climbed hillock and is washed on one side by the navigable river Bacchiglione, and on the other it is surrounded by other equally delightful hills that convey the impression of a very big theater. . . . For this reason, it enjoys the loveliest views on all sides, some enclosed, some more distant, and others that end only at the horizon. Loggias have been constructed on all four sides." This was how Andrea di Pietro della Gondola, known universally as Palladio, described the marvelous landscape that

provides the setting for his most celebrated, stunningly conceived villa in his 1570 treatise, *I Quattro Libri dell'Architettura* (The Four Books of Architecture). His efforts to blend the construction into the surrounding landscape are still, fortunately, very evident today. There have been very few subsequent intrusions into the countryside that provide the setting so crucially important for Palladio's buildings. This memorable location is exploited to the fullest by the architect and devoted to Naturgenuss, or delight in nature, the aristocratic visual cognizance that here embraces the radiance of a palpably real landscape, "with flowery meadows and very sunny fields," dispelling the "melancholic" shade that undermines serenity of the spirit.

La Rotonda is the Palladian building par excellence and one that has been most widely admired and copied. Toward the end of the eighteenth century, Johann Wolfgang von Goethe was much impressed by it on his first visit to Italy. "Today, I visited a splendid villa called La Rotonda, half an hour from the city, on a delightful hill. . . . Never, perhaps, has the art of architecture achieved such a degree of magnificence. . . . Just as the building may be admired in all its splendor from every part of the region, so, too, the view that can be enjoyed from it is of the finest. . . ." The villa stands in the midst of farmland like an acropolis, on top of a modest elevation deriving from a spur that descends from Monte Berico. La Rotonda is a belvedere, in the full sense of the word, open on all sides with four identical facades whose Ionic *pronaoi* are surmounted by tympanum panels. It dominates a glorious, natural, and almost circular amphitheater.

The construction brings together some of the recurring elements in Renaissance art, such as the ideal resolution of the centrally planned edifice, a leitmotiv in the work of the leading fifteenth and sixteenth century architects,

from Brunelleschi, Francesco di Giorgio Martini, Leonardo da Vinci, Bramante, Raphael, and Antonio da Sangallo to Baldassare Peruzzi. The volume of the building is underlined by the circular main hall and the axis of the dome, which the drawings in *I Quattro Libri dell'Architettura* portray as being higher to exercise its centripetal function. As Niklaus Pevsner wrote in his *An Outline of European Architecture*, here for the first time in western architecture the building is conceived as part of a whole with the countryside, not least by reason of its main axes, which extend into the natural environment and become part of it. Clearly, Palladio's lessons had been assimilated in 1725 by Richard Boyle, the third Earl of Burlington when designing his residence at Chiswick. This paradigm of the Palladian Revival was followed in the 1770s by Monticello, the villa built by Thomas Jefferson in an isolated part of central Virginia.

La Rotonda, on the outskirts of Vicenza and designed without any aspirations to farming, was included by Palladio among his "town houses" in his writings on architecture. Designed between 1565 and 1569 for Paolo

Almerico, a Vicenza gentleman and retired ecclesiastic, La Rotonda stands in an estate of twelve fields belonging to Almerico.

We know from the contract of sale dating from the period 1589 to 1591, before the building was completed by Vincenzo Scamozzi, that Almerico also owned 217 fields in the estates of Berga and Campadello. Palladio's patron had close links with the papal see, where he had held the important post of apostolic referendary to Pius IV and Pius V, and was steeped in classical culture. What he wanted was an edifice with exceptional symbolic and ceremonial value, a sort of Horatian country retreat that would at the same time embody the Palladian ideal of "seeing and being seen." In addition, the distancing of the villa's structure from the practical limitations of a utilitarian, productive nature, as James Ackerman observed, made it an ideal test bench for

the creativity both of the architect and his patron.

The edifice is a perfect exploitation of cube and sphere, reflected in the square and circle of the plan. A sort of architectural navel, an axis that sets itself at the center of its natural setting, La Rotonda was designed to be perceived as the summit of the hill on which it was built. Its solemn flights of steps follow and accentuate the gentle rhythm of the slope. The dome crowns the building just as the entire edifice crowns the hill. The elements from the classical idiom used in the architecture of the edifice are freed of the rigid orthodoxy of archeological associations to become an extension of the site's terrain. Like Andrea Palladio's other patrons, Paolo Almerico intended to create, in his country villa, a monument in praise of his own culture, taste, and personality. La Rotonda was to perpetuate across the centuries the greatness of Almerico's family and the dynastic pride of his stock. The dream, however, was fated to be short-lived. His son was to sell the villa and the surrounding land to the Capra family. At once, the scene and the focus changed. The inscription placed beneath the family crest by the new owners leaves little room for doubt, *MARIUS CAPRA / GABRIELIS F. // QUI AEDES HAS ARCTISSIMO / PRIMOGENITURAE / GRADUI SUBIECIT // UNA CUM OMNIBUS CENSIBUS / AGRIS VALLIBUS ET COLLI / BUS CITRA VIAM MAGNAM // MEMORIAE PEPETUAE MANDANS / HAEC DUM SUSTINET / AC ABSTINET*. The message proclaims the Capras' intention to renounce Almerico's beloved, classically inspired, intellectual *otium* (leisure), and his ambitions of family glory, to reassign to La Rotonda the much more traditional, less exalted, role of a country villa. No longer would it be a profane, secular monument, albeit one that may have been touched by the religious restlessness of the Reformation that found such fertile soil among the cultured Vicenza patricians of the mid sixteenth century. Now, it entered a new, more solid, and realistic dimension. Over the course of the seventeenth century, new owners would promote its economic value and rural functionality, albeit without modifying its original ethereal, isolated, configuration. The agricultural buildings were designed by Vincenzo Scamozzi, Palladio's most important immediate follower, and constructed on a lower level to be hidden from view, leaving the field clear for the pure, noble volume of the master's creation.

The stupendous dome that crowns the main hall. The frescoes are by Alessandro Maganza. The interlocking circles and squares, designed by Palladio to comply with arithmetical and musical ratios, hint at the philosophical and artistic coteries that met at the villa.

Thus, La Rotonda embodies two very different, contrasting aspirations. Conceived as a *panopticon* looking out over nature and the landscape, and the haven of a sophisticated nobleman inured to the splendor and intrigue of the papal court, it was a symbol of grandeur recovered from the pages of Vitruvius, and reinterpreted in a modern idiom, elements like the dome and front of the classical temple. Subsequently, it was converted to espouse the ethics of Sancta Agricoltura propounded by Alvise Cornaro, in compliance with the agrarian reform imposed in the Venetian States during the sixteenth century.

On the four pediments and the balustrades of the wide sweeping steps are statues in the classical style by Giambattista Albanese and Lorenzo Rubini, the brother-in-law and follower of the great Alessandro Vittoria, a close collaborator of Palladio's at Villa Barbaro at Maser. The refined stuccoes decorating the villa's fireplaces, created by Barto-lomeo Ridolfi, come from the same milieu. The reception rooms, too, are adorned with elegant stucco decoration by Rubini, Ruggero Bascapè, and Domenico Fontana. In 1978, the interiors were the setting for some memorable sequences from British director Joseph Losey's version of Mozart's *Don Giovanni*, shot in a dreamlike, exquisitely Palladian, Veneto. They were decorated subsequent to the original construction in several stages that did not always comply with the sober architectural concept. We should mention the frescoes by Anselmo Canera and the dome with its painted decoration by Alessandro and Giambattista Maganza, whereas the heroic architectural perspectives framing agitated figures were drawn by the brush of the French artist, Ludovico Dorigny, who specialized in illusionistic and theatrical effects for ceilings. He was very active in the late seventeenth and early eighteenth centuries in the *palazzi* on the lagoon and mainland residences of the Venetian aristocracy. The chapel, which stands apart from the other buildings, has been attributed to Carlo Borella. Today, the villa belongs to the noble Valmarana family, an ancient and prestigious house of the Vicenza aristocracy, who look after the elegant edifice with immense care and dedication.

VILLA VALMARANA AI NANI
VICENZA, VENETO

Facing:
The entrance hall at Villa Valmarana is decorated with several frescoes by Giambattista Tiepolo. The one illustrated dates from 1757, and relates Homer's sad story of the *Sacrifice of Iphigenia*.

Below left:
Villa Valmarana was built between 1665 and 1670 by a Venetian jurisconsult, Giovanni Maria Bertolo, as a pleasure lodge in which to enjoy the delights of country life.

Below right:
Giambattista Tiepolo: detail of the fresco in the entrance hall.

In the hills that crowd around the ancient city of Vicenza, not far from Palladio's Rotonda, there stands Villa Valmarana ai Nani. Like the celebrated sixteenth-century masterpiece, Villa Valmarana still belongs today to the long-established patrician family and was originally built as a residence and had no connection at all with farming or agricultural production. The villa was erected on the gentle slopes in the second half of the seventeenth century by the Venetian jurisconsult, Giovanni Maria Bertolo, a noted intellectual who gave his magnificent collection of books to the city of Vicenza, creating the nucleus of the library that still bears his name. The complex, built for the owner's relaxation and for the enjoyment of country living, comprises three separate units.

The original nucleus, the building that closes the courtyard on the north side, dates from 1669. It was probably the work of the Lugano architect, Antonio Muttoni, a member of a creative milieu that drew distantly on the heritage of the Romanesque Comacine and Campionese masters who worked on a number of important cathedrals in the Middle Ages. In the seventeenth and eighteenth centuries, their disciples included a number of crucial figures in Venetian art, including the baroque stucco artist, Abbondio Stazio, and later his rocaille-oriented pupil, Carpoforo Mazzetti, known as *Tencalla*.

The sober, Palladian lines of the earliest building are grafted onto a pronounced plinth formed by a balustrade-enclosed terrace around the

piano nobile, which is reached by a central flight of steps. Five simply framed rectangular apertures grace the facade, arranged in parallel rows and grouped in the center. The upper ones are less elaborate whereas the lower ones, with projecting architraves, are larger. Two single-light windows, set well apart on each side, complete the prospect. The *acroteria* of the short tympanum crowning the facade are decorated with statues that are replicated on the rear prospect.

Facing:
The *Stanza dell'Orlando Furioso* (Orlando Furioso Room) was frescoed by Giambattista Tiepolo to *quadratura* perspective drawings by Gerolamo Mengozzi Colonna. The modesty and restraint that we are told characterized the likely patron, Leonardo Valmarana, would help to explain the distinctly understated architectural solutions adopted for the residence, and the literary themes chosen for Tiepolo's fresco decorations in the main building.

Below:
Detail from the fresco in the *Stanza dell'Iliade*, or Iliad Room, showing Eurybates and Talthybius taking Briseis to Agamemnon.

In 1720, the property was acquired by the *conti*, or counts, Valmarana, one of Vicenza's leading families, who commissioned the guest quarters in the center. It is a *barchessa*-style annex marked off by seven arches on ashlar columns and joined to a vast entrance hall by a Tuscan order colonnade. The Valmaranas were also responsible for the three-aisle stables on the south side, which brings a greater sense of completeness to the complex.

Right and center:
Two frescoes in the *Stanza del Padiglione Gotico* in the *foresteria*, or guest quarters. Two richly dressed young women in exotically cut attire scrutinize a third woman.

Below right:
Detail of a fresco by Giandomenico Tiepolo in the *Stanza Cinese* (Chinese Room).

Below:
The *Stanza del Padiglione Gotico* (Gothic Pavilion Room) in the *foresteria* at Villa Valmarana ai Nani is decorated with frescoes by Giandomenico Tiepolo.

The probable designer of the last two buildings was Francesco Muttoni, the son of Antonio, who today is preferred to Giorgio Massari as the likely author of the final overall configuration. The villa's intriguing and widely known name, "ai Nani," or The Dwarfs, comes from the eighteen statues completed by Giovanni Battista Bendazzoli after about 1765. They are set on the surrounding wall, which is banded in rusticated ashlar. Although the architectural face presented by the various component parts of Villa Valmarana does not comprise a homogeneous whole, nor is it particularly successful, the residence does possess a trump card that has secured it lasting fame over the centuries. Actually, there are two trump cards, in the shape of the fresco cycles executed in 1757 by the great Giambattista Tiepolo and his son Giandomenico, respectively in the rooms of the original *palazzina* and in the *foresteria*, or guest quarters. Both artists were supported by the *quadraturista* Gerolamo Mengozzi, known as *Il Colonna*, who painted the trompe l'oeil architectural settings. Two very distinct, different, pictorial visions and worldviews, and two mature artistic personalities, confront each other. "Today, I saw Villa Valmarana, which Ticpolo adorned giving full rein to all his virtues and his shortcomings. His sublime style does not come across as natural, but there are some superb things. As a decorative artist in general, he is full of genius and resource." These were Johann Wolfgang von Goethe's observations when, on his first trip to Italy in 1787, he visited Villa Valmarana, by then a mandatory stop for sophisticated Grand Tourists from France, Great Britain, and central Europe arriving in the final days of the Ancien Régime. As Goethe noted, there are "virtues and shortcomings" in Giambattista Tiepolo, the artist of the dying glory of Europe's great royal courts, and tireless explorer of special effects. His qualities included a shrewd empiricism, vast imagination and freedom of spirit, extraordinary technical gifts, caprice, a sense of theater, and

Right:
The pastel-toned trompe l'oeil decoration in the *Stanza delle Scene di Carnevale* (Room of Carnival Scenes) includes a Moor carrying a tray of chocolate upstairs. It is widely attributed to Giambattista Tiepolo.

Following pages:
Giambattista Tiepolo may have preferred mythological themes for his frescoes at Villa Valmarana but his son, Giandomenico, seems to have been attracted by country scenes. Here we see a detail from the work depicting a peasant family at table in the *Stanza delle Scene Campestri* (Room of Rural Scenes).

work, has written, Tiepolo was a painter who ". . . set in motion a formidable pictorial strategy to attract and retain the observer's eye, rewarding it with a feast of visual emotions." Endlessly inventive, noted Cesare Brandi in his *Disegno della Pittura Italiana* (The Pattern of Italian Painting), Tiepolo created "images incarnate in light, founded on a range of pure, creamy, or barely modulated whites, each figure laced with luminescence and transparency, as if it were burgeoning while still in the grace and dampness of birth, in a space ignorant of gravity. . . privileged with. . . weightlessness. . . ."

Tiepolo was working here in Vicenza in 1757, shortly before the journey that would take him to Spain in late 1761, after he had finished the magnificent ceiling exalting the Pisani family at their luxurious villa at Strà. He was summoned to the Iberian peninsula by King Charles III of Bourbon to apply his talents to the Royal Palace in Madrid, where the artist died in 1770. Giambattista left for Spain accompanied by his sons, Giandomenico and Lorenzo, both painters like their father. Giambattista's marriage to Cecilia Guardi, sister of the celebrated painters, produced nine children, but only Giandomenico fashioned a distinctive artistic personality of his own. Giambattista Tiepolo's legend survived his death, particularly among other artists. Canova was a keen collector of Tiepolo's drawings while Francisco Goya considered him his benchmark, and continued the dialogue with his sons Giandomenico and Lorenzo (the latter remained in Madrid after their father's death). At Villa Valmarana, both Tiepolos were able to give full vent to their expression, revealing their two very different personalities. Giambattista represented the farthest, brilliant, frontier of baroque. Immersed in his dreams of mythology and sixteenth-century literary themes, he filled the walls of the *palazzina* with heroes and sculpturesque Olympian divinities. His lustrous, dream-inspired brushstroke revisited the pages of Ludovico Ariosto's *Orlando Furioso* and Torquato Tasso's *Jerusalem Delivered*. In contrast, the episodes from the *Iliad* and the *Aeneid* have a sweeping, more spectacular, impact. The *Sacrifice of Iphigenia* in the entrance hall seems to burst through the wall. Its trompe l'oeil Palladian atrium, featuring paired Ionic columns, is packed with figures in classical dress under a coffered ceiling. The *Stanza dell'Eneide*, the Aeneid Room, relates prodigies from Virgil's epic, like the scene of *Aeneas Introducing Cupid*

rhetorical force. Tiepolo's pictorial skills, as we can read between the lines of Goethe's diary, were far removed from the new ideals of sobriety and ethical concision that neoclassical Europe, daughter of the Enlightenment and as yet unshaken by the French Revolution, had embraced as her own. The artist Giambattista Tiepolo had a shining imagination and a spectacular grasp of light and beauty. As Adriano Mariuz, one of the most profound connoisseurs of his

Above:
Again in the *Stanza delle Scene Campestri*, Giandomenico frescoed the *Peasants' Repose*, set under the shady branches of a tree while a woman spins in silence.

Facing:
Not far from the village, a woman selling eggs rests against a tree trunk. Overhead, birds wheel among white summery clouds. Giandomenico Tiepolo, *Stanza delle Scene Campestri.*

Dressed as Ascanius to Dido, evoking the golden age of art for Giambattista, the Venetian *Seicento*, and Paolo Veronese in particular. In the *foresteria*, Giandomenico Tiepolo brought to life a more accessible, serenely domestic universe, elegantly tinged with melancholy. *Et in Arcadia Ego. . .* was an early Romantic Arcadia veined with a delicate, dark Schubertian melancholy. Scenes of country life, dancing in the open air, and nobles strolling like theatrical extras in bizarre, bulky costume offer a meditation on the imminent dissolution of the world they knew. There are also gypsies and charlatans, as well as chinoiseries, exotic details, and picturesque landscapes jostling precisely characterized local scenes featuring geometrical rows of mulberry trees, lofty oaks, and delightful villages. Giandomenico is "milky and succinct," as Cesare Brandi again would have it, "gently watering down his father's style to achieve an attractive figure of theatrical art in his harlequinesque decorations for the *foresteria* at Villa Valmarana. We seem to observe a collateral line, with respect to the father, one that is not legitimate." The *Stanza del Padiglione Gotico*, or Gothic Pavilion Room, where he worked with the *quadraturista* Gerolamo Mengozzi Colonna, has an elaborate architectural setting that anticipates the enormous popularity in the nineteenth century of the Gothic revival.

At Villa Valmarana, there is also space for chinoiseries in the *Stanza Cinese*, and for a final bittersweet look at the dying years of the Most Serene Republic in the fresco of the Charlatan in the *Stanza delle Scene di Carnevale*, or Room of Carnival Scenes. It is an artistic essay that seems to anticipate the celebrated *Mondo Novo* painted in the country *casino*, or pleasure lodge, near Venice of the Zianigo family from 1791 to 1793. Today, the entire wall fresco cycle is held at the Ca' Rezzonico Museum in Venice. All this was going on while slowly, imperceptibly, the curtain was falling on the revolutionary century of rococo and scientific discoveries. The old order was breaking up and the apparently unshakable status quo of absolute monarchy was cracking under the strain. When the Bastille fell on July 14, 1789, the aristocratic "century of the smile," as Mario Praz called it, vanished without trace to make way for the new bourgeois order. A little later, "the century that became bored with smiling was cured by Plutarch, and by Robespierre."

PALAZZO PITTI
FLORENCE, TUSCANY

The most magnificent of all Florence's *palazzi*, Palazzo Pitti spreads its gigantic rustic ashlar-work bulk across eight acres of the Boboli hill. For centuries, it was a Medici palace then, in the eighteenth century, it passed to the Lorraines. Subsequently, it became the residence of the Savoys in the years when Florence was the capital of Italy (1865–70). The fabric of the building preserves the marks, and the histories, of the dynasties that have lived there, revealing the various political stances and intellectual tastes that informed several crucial centuries of European culture. The *palazzo* was acquired by the Medici family when it

designs by Leon Battista Alberti, began work on plans drawn up by Filippo Brunelleschi around 1440.

The patron was banker Luca Pitti, the ally (and later enemy) of the Medicis in that family's ineluctable rise to power at Florence. Building work was suspended in 1470 when funds ran out and also because of the checkered fortunes of the owner, who was involved with the anti-Medici faction. The final plan featured a ground floor with three main gates, alternating with small, high rectangular windows. The two upper floors were each to have seven broad windows reaching down to floor level

was purchased by Eleonora of Toledo, the sophisticated daughter of the Viceroy of Naples and spouse of Duke Cosimo I. Her portrait was painted by Agnolo Bronzino in 1549. The construction of Palazzo Pitti, however, begun about a century earlier, in 1457, when Luca Fancelli, the implementer of a number of

Right:
Work on Palazzo Pitti began in 1457 under the architect Luca Fancelli. The building was extended by Bartolomeo Ammannati for the Medici family a century later.

Above:
The main facade of the *palazzo* in rusticated ashlar stonework stands out against the slopes of the Boboli hill.

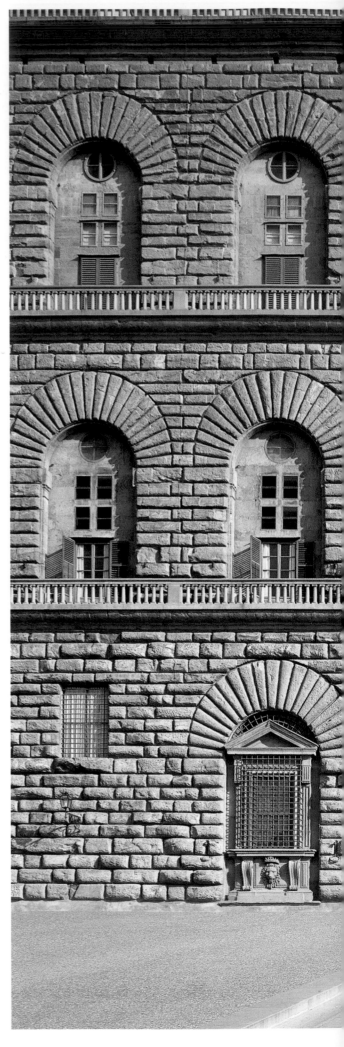

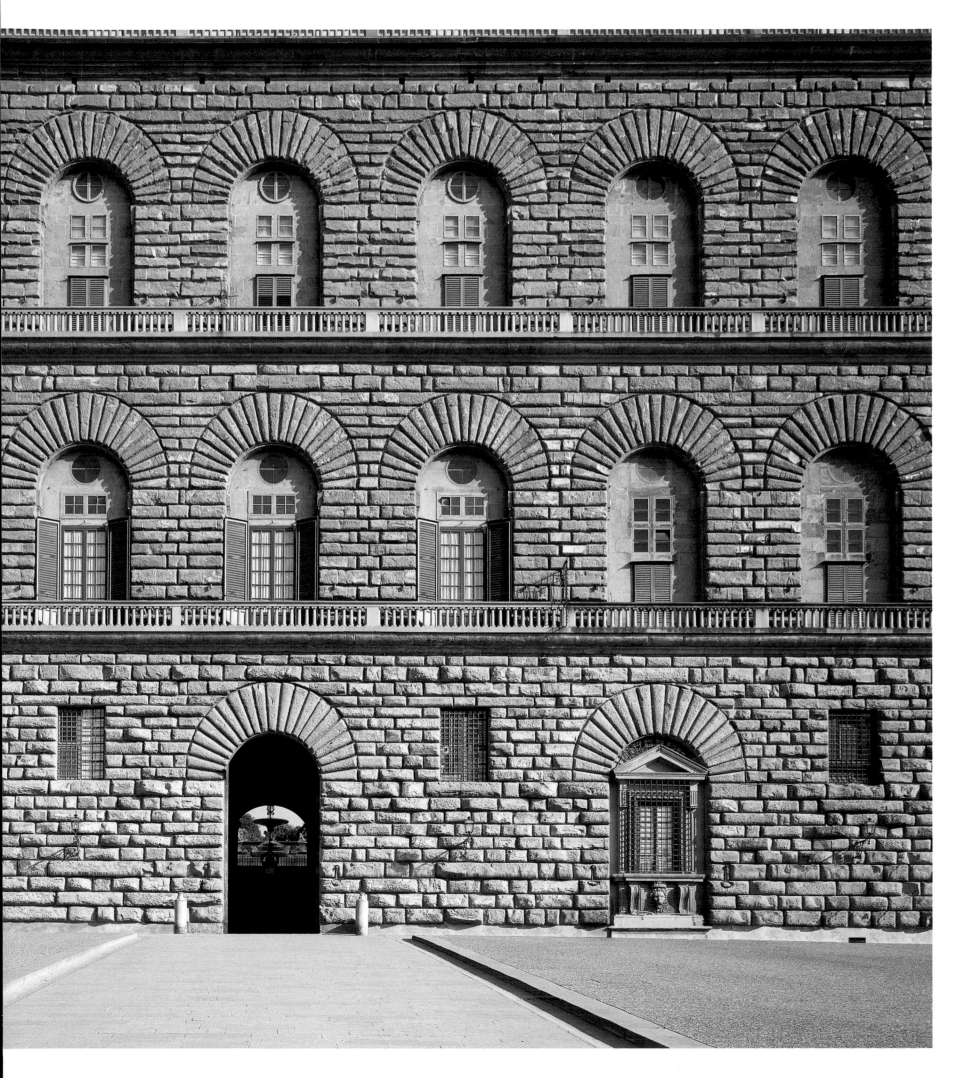

and linked by a continuous external balcony. At the top of the building was a low portico. Between 1558 and 1577, the Medicis installed themselves on the ducal throne with the imperial blessing of Charles V. The family began extending the *palazzo*, commissioning Ammannati, who made two huge openings in the side gates to focus attention on the magnificent courtyard. From 1620, the architect Giulio Parigi was active on the main facade, adding three more windows on each side. Twenty years later, it was his son Alfonso who made a further extension of the first and second floors, giving the front its present-day appearance. Its superb facade is 673 feet long and 118 feet high, comprising three floors, each with a columned balustrade. In compliance with classical canons, the imposing rustic ashlar is more restrained on the upper stories. Eleven arcades enclose elegant tympanum-surmounted windows, their parapets adorned with the crowned head of a lion, the symbol of Florence, between their brackets. On the second floor, there are twenty-three arcades, and thirteen on the third. Florence was highly conservative, remaining faithful to Renaissance models, even in the seventeenth century, as late mannerism made way for the new frontiers of baroque. As a result, the Brunelleschian architectural style of the original building was maintained. The materials selected were also inevitably those that had been adopted for the ancient structure. Finally, when the house of Lorraine was ruling, Giuseppe Ruggieri built the two porticoed and terraced outer

Facing:
The frescoes in the *Sala di Giovanni da San Giovanni* tell how the Muses came to seek refuge in Tuscany after being driven from Parnassus. In the photograph, Pegasus is being bitten by small monsters while the blind Homer is about to fall from the balcony into the room itself.

Below:
One of the rooms in the Silver Museum on the ground floor. It is adjoined by other independent sections: the Porcelain Museum, the Carriage Museum, and the Costume Gallery. This stupendous Baroque cabinet, known as the *Stipo d'Alemagna*, was made at Augsburg and donated to Grand Duke Ferdinando II de'Medici to Archduke Leopold of Tyrol in 1628.

projecting wings, the so-called *rondò*, then Pasquale Poccianti made further contributions in 1746 and from 1783 to 1819. Meanwhile, Gaspare Maria Paoletti was busy in the Meridiana pavilion area, which stretches towards Boboli and was completed by Poccianti in the early nineteenth century. In 1840, the same neoclassical architect renovated the atrium of the *palazzo* with Doric columns and installed a new staircase that was named after him.

In 1860, Palazzo Pitti became the property of the Italian crown and the official residence of Vittorio Emanuele II. The king was a bluff, direct Piedmontese, and a keen hunter who loved the outdoor life. He was more at home at Villa La Petraia in the company of his *Bela Rusin*, or in a pavilion in the gardens of Boboli, than in the reception rooms of the palace itself among the lavish furnishings, gilded ornaments, and artistic masterpieces. In 1919, Vittorio Emanuele III donated Palazzo Pitti to the Italian state, along with the Medici Villas of Castello, La Petraia and Poggio a Caiano. Included in the gift were the private ornaments and furnishings the Savoys had made for the various grand-ducal residences during the court's five-year stay in Tuscany.

Palazzo Pitti is the home of the Palatine Gallery, the Gallery of Modern Art, the Silver Museum, which brings together the best of the exquisite curiosities of the Medicis' *Wunderkammer*, and the Carriage Museum. Its solemn courtyard was completed by Bartolomeo Ammannati during the restructuring work that went

Above:
A lapis lazuli, gold, and gilt bronze flask made by Bernardo Buontalenti and Giovanni Biliverti in 1583.

Left:
One wall of the *Sala di Giovanni da San Giovanni*, named for the noted artist who painted the frescoes for the wedding of Grand Duke Ferdinando II and Vittoria della Rovere in 1635. After Giovanni's death, the work was completed by Ottavio Vannini, Francesco Furini, and Cecco Bravo.

Below:
Two finely worked mother-of-pearl and gilt silver cups that were probably brought to Florence from the Low Countries. The pair dates from the late sixteenth century.

Francesco del Tadda and Francesco Susini. At the base of the fountain is the seventeenth-century *Grotta di Mosè* (Moses' Cave), with an elliptical tank, behind which stands the colossal statue of the biblical patriarch. The statue was created from an ancient torso in porphyry by Raffaello Curradi and completed by Cosimo Salvestrini.

The Palatine Gallery boasts paintings from a range of Italian and other schools from the fifteenth to the eighteenth centuries. The incredible array includes masterpieces of painting, eighteenth-century illusionistic frescoes by Pietro da Cortona, Ciro Ferri, Poccetti, and Volterrano, baroque furnishings inlaid with hard stones from the Opificio in Florence, classical sculptures and busts, damasks and silk brocades, sumptuous cabinets, Sèvres porcelain, Imari *potiches* (vases), gilt consoles, Roman cups, tapestries, and sixteenth- and seventeenth-century portraits of the Medicis by the Dutch artists Pourbous and Suttermans. The Lorraines, especially Ferdinando III (during the restoration and after the bequest made by Anna Maria Luisa) continued to add to the decoration of the rooms. The Palatine Elector and the last of the Medicis, Anna Maria Luisa made an inalienable donation to the city of Florence on her death in 1743 of all the family's art collections. The Lorraine contributions also continued after the ravages of the Napoleonic period. It is impossible even to list the names of all the artists represented in the Gallery, which includes Raphael, Filippo Lippi, Andrea del Sarto, Fra' Bartolomeo, Titian, Tintoretto, Paolo Veronese, Rubens, Guercino, and Velazquez, as well as Ridolfo del Ghirlandaio, Sebastiano del Piombo, Pontormo, Agnolo Bronzino, Federico Barocci, Artemisia Gentileschi, Cristofano Allori, Giovanni Bilivert, the great seventeenth-century Florentine artists, *Il Cigoli*, Carlo Dolci, Lorenzo Lippi, and Matteo Rosselli. Neoclassicism is also represented, for example in the splendid *Venus Italica* by Antonio Canova, completed in 1810 and donated to the Uffizi by Napoleon. The same idiom informs the sophisticated rooms created by Giuseppe Cacialli, such as the *Gabinetto Rotondo* (Round Room) and the *Bagno* (Bathroom) of Maria Luisa of Bourbon, queen of Etruria in the early nineteenth century. The Royal Apartments emphasize even more clearly the sense of opulence in the residence of the former autocratic rulers of Tuscany, of the Lorraines and finally of the Savoy kings, the last tenants being Umberto I with

on from 1558 to 1570. Closed on three sides by the internal facade and wings of the building, and on the fourth by a terraced ground floor, the courtyard features three orders of ashlar, engaged columns, between which are the arcades of the portico at ground level, and on the two upper floors by large windows or balconies, surmounted by imposing entablatures. The structural rustication of Palazzo Pitti is a bold innovation. The courtyard is conceived as a linking element between the facade overlooking the *piazza* and the Boboli gardens to the rear. On the terrace is the *Fontana del Carciofo*, or Artichoke Fountain, by

Above:
Portrait of Valdemar Christian, prince of Denmark. The painting is by the Flemish artist Justus Sustermans, court painter to the Medicis from 1619 to his death.

Facing:
Sala di Marte in the Palatine Gallery. The ceiling fresco is by Pietro da Cortona.

Following pages:
Sala di Giove: Left, the *Portrait of a Lady*, known as the *Veiled Lady*, painted by Raphael about 1516. *Right*, the *Four Philosophers* by Pieter Paul Rubens, dating from 1611 or 1612.

Pages 148 and 149:
The *Sala di Apollo* has a wealth of masterpieces, including Andrea del Sarto's *Pietà* and the *Portrait of Charles I of England with Queen Henrietta of France* by Anton van Dyck.

when Marquis Giorgini in the 1950s organized the first shows that sealed the success of Emilio Pucci, Roberto Capucci, Fabiani, and Simonetta.

Palazzo Pitti is haunted by the unquiet spirits of the last saturnine, eccentric, baroque Medicis, portrayed in shades of public pomp and private misery by Harold Acton and Anna Banti. The overweight Cosimo III, obsessed with piety and ceremony, and his spouse, the beautiful and neurotic Marguerite Louise d'Orleans, a proud *fille de France* raised at the young Louis XIV's court at Versailles, felt constricted by Florence's narrow Counter-Reformation horizons. Their ghosts are joined by those of their children, the restless, ill-starred Grand Prince Ferdinando, the gentle but shrewd Violante of Bavaria, and the deranged, stuttering Giangastone, last of the grand dukes from the house of Medici.

The Boboli garden, which covers more than eleven acres, starts at the hill behind the *palazzo*'s facade and rises to Forte Belvedere, extending as far as Porta Romana and offering one of the finest, and most typical, examples of an Italian garden. On the cusp of mannerism and the nascent baroque, the Boboli was laid out at the behest of Eleonora of Toledo by *Il Tribolo,* in 1550, the year in which the artist died. Work continued under Ammannati, and then Buontalenti in 1583,

Facing:
On the terrace facing the Boboli Gardens is the famous *Fontana del Carciofo*, the Artichoke Fountain, a seventeenth-century work by Francesco del Tadda and Francesco Susini.

Above and right:
Details of the Boboli Gardens. The statue of Perseus rising from the waters and the so-called Goat Gate leading to the *Giardino di Madama*.

Queen Margherita and Vittorio Emanuele III. The assemblage of furniture from several periods evinces a typically nineteenth-century air of formality. Again there is a hogdepodge of dynastic portraits, mirrors, drapes, door curtains, Florentine, Gobelins, and Beauvais tapestries, Empire fauteuils and consoles, superb paintings by Guido Reni, Titian, Giovanni Battista Lampi, and Charles Lebrun. Next to the throne room is the famously elegant ballroom, better known as the *Sala Bianca*, or White Room. Dating from 1776 to 1780, this neoclassical ambience was designed by Gaspare Maria Paoletti with stuccoes by the Lugano-born Albertolli brothers. It was the birthplace of Italian fashion,

of Caracalla and an Egyptian obelisk bearing the name of the pharaoh Sesostri. Both were unearthed by the Medicis during excavations at Rome. The amphitheater was the appointed venue for the feasts and elaborate performances beloved of the court at Florence, the city where the Camerata de' Bardi developed the art of *recitar cantando*, the melodrama. Further is the *Vivaio di Nettuno*, a wide basin in the middle of which sits a rock surrounded by tritons and mermaids. On top stands the bronze statue of the sea god himself, cast in 1565 by Stoldo Lorenzi.

It has three spaces inside, revealing the ceaseless, ambiguous transformations of the mannerist canon. In the first, we leave behind Vasari's portico and the two statues by Bandinelli and gaze on stuccoed walls depicting human and animal figures, an allusion to the myth of Deucalion and Pyrrha's escape from the Flood. Trompe l'oeil paintings simulate trellises with birds and a collapsed vault, from which curious satyrs and wild animals peek out amid garlands of spontaneous plants. On either side, Michelangelo's *Prigioni* have been substituted by copies. Set in a texture of

to be concluded in the seventeenth century by Alfonso Parigi and others. The Boboli sweeps up the hill, offering a panoramic view of Florence's cityscape from its magnificent fountains, myriad sculptures, Roman funeral stones, urns, luscious vegetation, and the pattern of box hedges that transform it into a virtual extension of the Medici palace. The seventeenth-century amphitheater is stunning, focusing attention on the ancient gray granite basin from the Baths

The park also includes a supremely eighteenth-century feature, the bizarre domed pavilion of the Kaffcchaus, erected by Zanobi del Rosso in 1776 for the Lorraines. If we briefly glance back to the sixteenth century, Giorgio Vasari will tell us that Eleonora of Toledo loved grottoes, the *pièce de résistance* of any mannerist garden, and that she had hired Baccio Bandinelli to create one "full of tartars and sponges frozen by the water." But far and away the most extraordinary grotto in the Boboli is the masterpiece of the mannerist imaginative vocabulary created by Buontalenti from 1583 to 1593.

crystals and sponges, they are swathed in jets of water and enhanced by artful lighting effects. The centerpiece of the second room is the marble group of *Paris and Helen*, by Vincenzo de' Rossi, while the third was once embellished by ornamental fountains, luminous reflections, water features, and rare plants. It is dominated by the sinuous beauty of the bathing *Venus* by Giambologna, carved in 1570 and set over a basin with four monstrous, lascivious satyrs clinging to its base.

Facing:
Some of the many statues that grace the Boboli Gardens.

This page:
Views of the *Grotta del Buontalenti*, where materials are transformed into the shapes of living creatures. Metamorphosis was one of the favorite themes of mannerists.

Villa di Chigi al Cetinale

Siena, Tuscany

In the middle decades of the nineteenth century and the first half of the twentieth, an eccentric, cultured Anglo-American elite came to live in the hills of Tuscany. Its members restored ancient buildings, dreaming of some lost golden age of ideal beauty and elegance. The residences involved in the efforts of this expatriate community included Lady Sybil Cuffe Cutting's Villa Medici, Vernon Lee's

The effortless nonchalance, subtle British humor, and "ordinary" lifestyle of the last resident at Cetinale, Lord Lambton, and his desire to enjoy this ancient, history-soaked structure without allowing himself to be overawed, is far removed from the mummified museum-like atmosphere that often enshrouds other ancient noble houses. The direct, informal mood is reflected in the Latin

Above:
The long, cypress-lined avenue that leads from Villa di Cetinale's front elevation. The exterior of the villa was probably designed by the Roman architect Carlo Fontana, a pupil of Gian Lorenzo Bernini.

Ombrellino, I Tatti, from which Bernard Berenson, the fearsome "B.B.," reigned over the world of international art, and the castle of Montegufoni, where the sophisticated Sitwell siblings commissioned a fresco cycle on the commedia dell'arte from Severini. In a sense, the rebirth of Villa Chigi al Cetinale sprang from the same impassioned urge to recover the past that turn-of-the-century residents in Tuscany shared.

inscription on the wall of the second-floor loggia. "Whoever you are, newcomer, what to you may seem horrible, to me is beautiful. Stay if you like it. Go if it displeases you. I will be grateful to you in either case." This eloquent declaration of intent was ordered by cardinal Flavio Chigi, nephew of Alexander VII, who was elected to the papal throne in 1655. The pontiff, whose given name was Fabio Chigi, belonged to a noble Siena family that had achieved a position of eminence at the Roman court a century earlier in the person of banker Agostino Chigi, the friend and patron of Raphael. Agostino had accumulated enormous wealth by trading in alum from the mines at Tolfa, for which he held the monopoly.
The villa stands at Ancaiano, near

Sovicille, on the very spot where the future pope was born. However, it was his nephew, Cardinal Flavio, the contradictory child of a century torn between baroque sensuality and the penitent spirit of the Counter-Reformation, who built the villa from an old farmhouse in the middle of one of the many family estates in the area. It was Flavio who commissioned the plans from the Roman architect Carlo Fontana, a pupil of Gianlorenzo Bernini. Fontana was frequently used by the Chigis for their buildings in Rome and around Siena, where he designed Palazzo Chigi Zondadari at San Quirico d'Orcia. Work dragged on from 1675 to 1678, continuing later until 1716, under the supervision of Bonaventura Chigi Zondadari. The

This page:
Some views of the villa's magnificent gardens. The formal garden has been laid out to a highly idiosyncratic Anglo Italian formula that juxtaposes classic box and yew hedges with old garden roses and wisteria.

Following pages: A view of the main facade from the front.

resulting edifice is in a geometrically configured fifteenth-century idiom, which takes as its model the work of the Siena architect Baldassarre Peruzzi, in particular. Two projecting avant-corps grace the main facade, which is decorated with the Chigi and della Rovere crests. They frame the main building, which is set farther back, and decorated with two three-arch loggias set one on top of the other. The upper loggia was subsequently walled up and converted into a closed room. It is still spiritually connected to the surrounding landscape by its nineteenth-century trompe l'oeil decoration, which sweeps away the walls to present verdant

landscapes and clear, turquoise skies filled with soaring birds. After building was complete, the cardinal went on to deal with arrangements outside, which again were probably executed by Fontana. A single axis of symmetry seems to have been created at Cetinale. It divides in two the building and the gardens around it, continuing in front along the avenue lined with polled holm oaks that first descends, and then climbs the hill facing the villa. To the rear of the main building, the axis extends along another avenue, much of it flanked by cypresses. It emerges from the villa through a sort of monumental gateway with brickwork side elements, decorated with classical busts, obelisks, and niches with statues of prisoners, finally arriving at the vast *piazzale*, or open space, at the foot of the hill. The statues may be the work of Giuseppe Mazzuoli, who we know was engaged after 1680 to produce a large number of classically inspired sculptures for Villa

Chigi's *piazzale* and long avenue. However, most of the statues were subsequently destroyed or moved elsewhere.

The *piazzale* is the starting point for the superbly scenic brick stairs that lead to the Romitorio. The great statue of Hercules erected on the flat ground in 1687 may well be the focal point of a symbolic itinerary that gradually shakes off the temptations of the profane and moves closer to the sacred. This is represented by the several story-high Romitorio, the cross on whose facade may be a *memento mori*, or reminder of mortality. It is a holy scene, set in a solemn, theatrical space. This arrangement reveals the two sides of the cardinal's soul, which mingled religion with the pleasure-loving worldliness of a seventeenth-century aristocrat, embodied in the residence itself and the formal gardens around it. The Romitorio was inhabited until the late nineteenth century by twelve hermit friars, who once a month visited the chapel in the woods that stands at the top of two hundred steps. It became emblematic of the cathartic impulse, and sincere desire for spiritual renewal.

On the slopes of the hill beneath, in the midst of tight-packed oaks, is the mysterious Tebaide park, which adds another unusual element to the colorful history of the villa. This initiatory wood takes its name from the Thebaid, an inaccessible desert area in Upper Egypt where, in the third century A.D., many Christian anchorites retreated to lead an ascetic life, entirely devoted to prayer and contemplation. The Tebaide unfolds along an extended route of paths and avenues that are adorned with statues of saints and hermits. It is also the site of one of the seven votive chapels, dedicated to the sorrows of the Virgin Mary, arranged in a circle with Cetinale in the center.

Tradition has it that the sacred wood was planted by cardinal Flavio Chigi in expiation for the death of a rival in love. Other reports, backed up by reliable documentary sources, agree that the construction of the Tebaide and Romitorio took place after Flavio Chigi's death. These witnesses ascribe the bizarre statues of the *romiti* (hermits) or the *scherzi*, representations of animals in the rock, to Bartolomeo Mazzuoli, Giuseppe's younger relative. Bartolomeo was commissioned to work on the villa by Bonaventura Chigi Zondadari, Flavio Chigi's nephew and heir, in the early eighteenth century. Nevertheless, it is difficult to rule out the influence of the

cardinal's strong personality on the design of the Tebaide. Hermitages were popular in baroque Rome, as may be seen in the description of the city in 1687 and 1688 by the Swedish architect, Nicodemus Tessin. He mentions two, the one at the Palazzo of the *Connestabile* (Constable) Lorenzo Onofrio Colonna, the great friend of Flavio Chigi, and another at Palazzo Altieri, in Piazza del Gesù.

Toward the end of the seventeenth century, several editions of a Palio were run at Cetinale in a low-key imitation of the celebrated horse race at Siena. The extravagant monsters and animal figures sketched in the stone, and scattered in the undergrowth along the main path through the Tebaide, seem in fact to hint at the Siena Palio. The *Drago*

(Dragon), the *Tartuca* (Turtle), and the *Chiocciola* (Snail) symbolize the *contrade*, the districts of Siena, that bear those names. At the beginning of the seventeenth century, the villa was the perfect setting for extravagant social events. Not long built by Carlo Fontana for Flavio Chigi, it was at the center of a network of important relationships involving the Vatican and the court of Versailles, where the cardinal had held sensitive diplomatic positions when Louis XIV was on the throne. The prelate, a keen hunter in the forests of Montagnola, also built a theater, finished in 1688, at the end of the main avenue.

With the generous hand of Flavio Chigi at the helm, Cetinale was the setting for an intense round of entertaining and

Above:
The painting of the Virgin and Child is by Sano di Pietro, a Sienese artist who was active in the mid-fifteenth century.

Left:
The loggia on the second floor of the villa is dominated by the Latin inscription placed there by Cardinal Flavio Chigi, which recites "Whoever you are, you who have come here, what to you may look horrendous to me seems lovely. Stay if it pleases you. Go if it does not please you. In either case, I will be grateful to you."

Facing:
The dining room created by bricking in the upper loggia is linked to the surrounding landscape by the trompe l'oeil decoration added in the nineteenth century.

official events. Flavio frequently stayed at the villa, inviting distinguished guests and maintaining the Chigi family's links with the Sienese aristocracy from whose ranks they had emerged. Flavio himself was one of the leading figures on the Roman political and artistic scene. After his period as an ambassador at Versailles, he appears to have been unable to live without the magic of the theater. Carlo Fontana drew on Bernini's example to create entertainments and performances that used the stage as a machine for invention and realistic illusion. The show presented on the feast of the Ascension, on August 15, 1668 was a memorable, magical spectacle, held in the garden of Cardinal Chigi's Roman residence at Quattro Fontane. In early June 1691, at

the height of the very first, stupendous season at Cetinale, the grand duke of Tuscany himself came to call. The visit by the illiberal, luxury-loving Cosimo III was immortalized in a marble bas relief by Bartolomeo Mazzuoli in 1707. The work was placed in the villa's entrance hall. A private letter from the cardinal's sister, Agnesa Chigi, describes with barely concealed pride the sparkling *allegrie* (delights) that were planned to welcome the grand duke. "There will be plays. There will be Palios, ball games and *accademie* (musical entertainments)." It was a great honor, and an act of deference by the grand duke that was frequently mentioned in the many hagiographic descriptions of the event. The visit was a tribute that was, in a certain sense, due to Flavio's rank as a cardinal, and even more so to the enormous prestige that the Chigi family had by then achieved throughout Europe. Their ascent had begun in Siena two centuries earlier, burgeoning amid the splendors of Renaissance Rome, to culminate in the dazzling baroque glory of Alexander VII's election as pope. It was by kind permission of Grand Duke Cosimo that a fair was held each year on September 21, the feast of Saint Eustace, patron of the small church adjoining the residence where the saint's relics were kept. The fair was a major event, with "great attendance of local people and strangers." It was also the occasion for the Palio di Cetinale. This exceptional race was held seven times between 1679 and 1692.

Founded in 1531, when Siena's glory as an independent political force was about to end, the Congrega dei Rozzi was extremely active in both writing and producing new dramas, combining deliciously popular theatrical genres, such as "bucolic" plays, eclogues, and farces, with pastoral, or "Maytime", themes enacted by Arcadian nymphs and shepherds. The Rozzi became an *accademia* in 1690 and undoubtedly made good use of the open-air theatrers, the *teatri di verzura*, in the villas around Siena, where their talents were employed in "administering entertainment to the nobility with their humorous, light-hearted spectacles." Proof of this comes from Giuseppe Fabiani, in his history of the Accademia dei Rozzi, published in Siena in 1775. ". . . No less important were the Performances that they put on for other Princes and Lords, and especially in 1676 for the advent of His Excellence Don Austino Chigi, Prince of Farnese, Nephew of Alexander VII, in whose presence they

159

performed in that year at the Villa della Costa Fabbri, a sylvan work entitled *Interest Triumphs over Love*, written by academician Francesco Faleri, known as *L'Abbozzato*. The play had been presented four years previously by the Rozzi at the Teatro Grande in Siena." Austino was, of course, Agostino Chigi, the son of Alessandro VII's brother Augusto, whose marriage to Virginia Borghese created the powerful Roman branch of the family. His cousin, Flavio, was equally active, as Giovan Battista Bucalossi recalls when he describes a feast that took place in 1690 at Cetinale. The cardinal ". . . every Year would, on September 21, cause to be run a Palio delle Contrade della Città race. On that day, the Rozzi arrived in multitudinous procession with the Arcirozzo (head of the academy) to said Villa, where they were agreeably welcomed by His Excellency and served Him at table with Song, and in the Palio with a solemn Procession, after a bucolic Comedy entitled the *Marriage of Maca*, and at the

end with a pleasing Serenade." Another play organized at Cetinale by the Rozzi is mentioned in the deliberations of the academy for February 23, 1691, and a detailed account of a Palio that took place on September 17, 1692, has also survived.

The American writer, Edith Wharton, who visited Cetinale in the early twentieth century, confided to the owner, Marquis Chigi, that she was surprised how small the building was, considering its noble past. That did not stop her falling hopelessly in love with it. "The house at Cetinale is so charming, with its stately double flight of steps leading up to the first floor, and its monumental doorway opening on a central *salone*, that it may well be ascribed to the architect of San Marcello in Rome, and of Prince Lichtenstein's 'Garden Palace' in Vienna. . . . But the glory of Cetinale is its park." The park begins with the small garden with its formal parterres laid out in front of the facade. It is graced by topiary box hedges and embellished by the customary vases of citrus plants and generously flowered

seasonal blooms. The formal garden was reinterpreted by the lady of the house according to her own personal Anglo-Italian approach, which combined sculpted box and yew hedges, perfumed old garden roses and cascades of wisteria, adding colorful, freer, and more brilliant brushstrokes to the texture of blooms woven by the gardens on the left-hand side of the main residence. The vast area of parkland that climbs the hill in the opposite direction to the avenue of cypresses, added seventy years ago, is occupied by the Tebaide.

The villa's contemporary history began in 1977, when an aristocratic British couple acquired it and decided to rescue it from the state of decay into which it had declined. "What convinced us to take this step," Lord Lambton revealed to the writer a few years ago, "was a sort of fatal attraction for the Tebaide." It took only a few seasons for the ancient house to regain its former splendor. It was refurnished with valuable old family furnishings from Britain, locally made antiques, and an impressive collection of sculpture. After a disastrous fire, which destroyed several works of art, the main reception room again echoed, when I visited, to the joyous barks of the Lambtons' eight adopted dogs, draped comfortably on the long white sofas. There emerge from my memories two elaborate gilt consoles by William Kent, full of books and other objects, on either side of the Renaissance fireplace in *pietra serena* stone. I also remember French neoclassical *papier peint* panels, fifteenth-century statues and, in an exquisitely English touch of eccentricity, an eighteenth-century kennel, a masterpiece of micro-architecture in the Palladian idiom. The room was dominated by the small altarpiece of the *Virgin and Child* by Sano di Pietro, one of the elegant Sienese artists, so dear to Pius II, another pope born near here, who chose to imbue their art with petrified pictorial anachronism. The bedrooms provided equally unexpected exercises in style. Romantic chintz canopics, a Lucca-made *lit à la duchesse* (bed) from Villa Garzoni at Collodi, and Lord Lambton's George II four-poster bed jostled with Victorian Arts and Craft furniture, Pre-Raphaelite paintings, engravings by Joshua Reynolds, and rare sixteenth-century miniatures on parchment. In the kitchen, there were attractive seventeenth-century paintings *Hunter*, *Gardener*, and *Farmer*. Beyond the vast, bright entrance loggia, watched over by two massive statues of Roman matrons, the reception room on the

ground floor housed a huge eighteenth-century family portrait set between two baroque marble busts of popes Clement XI and Innocent XI. Other portraits depicting the Chigis, until recently the owners of Cetinale, were to be seen on the walls of the villa, bearing witness to the astonishing creative sap that has coursed through the residence, and through all the branches of the Chigi family tree, over centuries of power, pomp, intrigue, obstacles, and beauty.

VILLA
BIANCHI BANDINELLI
SIENA, TUSCANY

When Geggiano came into the possession of the noble Bianchi Bandinelli family from Siena in 1530, as part of the dowry of Gerolama Santi, it was a plain, fourteenth-century agricultural building with adjoining rooms. The present configuration, atop a low hill with a holm

off by pilasters and intersected on the second floor by a broad horizontal fascia that joins the parallel lines of the string course and those of the parapet under the windows. At the same time, work began on the lovely Italian garden, which was laid out on the far side of the forecourt in

Bandinelli and Chigi Zondadari crests, commemorating the two authors of the eighteenth-century makeover that transformed the villa's appearance forever. The diagonal walls feature two niches that house the allegorical statues of *Tragedy* and *Comedy*, by the Maltese sculptor Bosio. The perspective effect of the back of the stage is further emphasized by a cypress tree.

The garden is sheltered by a high wall with six strategically placed gates, flanked by monumental pillars surmounted by stepped pyramids. These in turn are embellished by "ancient," twin-handled urns, decorated by a meander, garlands, and mocking terracotta Rocaille Barbary apes. A classic feature inherited from the Mannerist and Baroque garden, the *Teatrino di Verzura* at Geggiano is exquisitely Rococo in style, and has a charmingly sophisticated agility reminiscent of Mozart. Added at a relatively late date with respect to the

oak-lined *cerchiaia* approach, took shape in 1768 to 1769. The original modest country residence, whose various elements had already been unified and extended with a second-floor room and loggias on the left side, was comprehensively renovated. As is often the case, the occasion was a prestigious matrimonial and dynastic alliance, this time between Anton Domenico Bianchi Bandinelli Paparoni and his second wife, the widowed Cecilia Chigi Zondadari, whose married name was Malavolti. The main frontage rose under the supervision of Anton Domenico, its features marked

front of the villa, known as the *piazzone*. The garden thus lies perpendicular to the residence. The green box parterre leads to the eighteenth-century *Teatrino di Verzura*, or Theater of Greenery, with its brick stage and high laurel hedge forming semicircular wings. At right angles to the axis that joins the villa to the theater is the line leading from the *selvatico*, or country scene, on one side to the herb garden and its elegant fishpond on the other. As the focal point of the garden, the theater has a proscenium in two sections. Its arches are crowned by classical pediments that flaunt the Bianchi

overall design of the garden, it was certainly complete by 1783, the year in which the visiting poet Vittorio Alfieri performed personally in one of his celebrated tragedies. The prestigious guest is emblematic of the cultural aspirations of the Bianchi Bandinelli family, whose traditional openness of mind has endured through the generations and the centuries down to the present day. The bedroom used by Alfieri is in the Louis Seize idiom. It was adorned with French wallpaper from the Au Grand Balcon company, with an engraving portraying the Asti-born poet's "bosom friend," Francesco Gori Gandellini, and some editions of Alfieri's works. The room survives, its furnishings intact, exactly as it was in 1780. Work, which was to last for a decade, also began in 1780 on the most original decorative repertoire in the residence.

These are the *Allegorie dei Mesi*, or Allegories of the Months, frescoed by the Tyrolean artist, Ignaz Moder, a traveling painter who considered himself Sienese by adoption.

Inspired by the drawings of Giuseppe Zocchi and the engravings of Francesco Bartolozzi, the Allegories of the Months blend the Rocaille style and new neoclassical elements to portray various aspects of rural life, with extremely interesting results. It is in some respects an eighteenth-century version of the celebrated *Mesi di Trento*, or Cycle of the Months, painted hundreds of years earlier at the Castello del Buonconsiglio in Trento by the Gothic master, Wenceslas of Bohemia. The Geggiano work interweaves nature's cyclical rhythms with a minuet of gallant episodes inspired by the Commedia dell'Arte. Nature and

Facing:
Two views of the *Saletta Azzurra* (Blue Room). The walls are decorated with eighteenth-century *papier peint* with a pattern of trophies set in arches. The elegant rococo furniture is also color-themed in tones of pale blue.

Below:
On the villa's second floor is the *Salottino Verde* (Green Room), flamboyantly adorned with mock-tapestry representations of rural tasks, set in extravagant rococo borders.

Left:
Detail of the door of the *Salottino Verde*. The scenes from country life echo the motifs and colors of the decoration on the ceiling.

theater come together in a uniquely impressive performance while the pictorial narrative involves what we might call "special guest stars," in the portraits of celebrated figures of the period. Subjects include the owners of the residence and patrons, Anton Domenico and Cecilia Bianchi Bandinelli, Anton Domenico's daughter from his first marriage and her husband, Filippo Sergardi, Alessandra Mari, an active participant in the anti-French Arezzo-based *Viva Maria* movement, and the famous musician and singer Perellino, who is portrayed with his actress daughters.

Another illustrious guest at Geggiano was Pius VI, who arrived in 1798 at the height of the Napoleonic wars. His elaborately framed portrait, in papal tiara and bearing the keys of Saint Peter, hangs over the headboard of the four-poster bed in the so-called *Stanza del Cardinale*, or Cardinal's Room, its walls decorated with graceful chinoiserie-themed *Toile de Jouy*, where the distinguished guest enjoyed his hours of rest. Geggiano's is an understated Settecento, very different from other, pretentiously academic versions lavish with pomp, large mirrors, and glittering gilt finishes. Here, we find elegant, more nuanced tones that simultaneously express joy and melancholy. At Geggiano, there is a sophisticated, ironic, decorative artifice, such as the grass shoots that mimic tapestries of seasonal agricultural

Above:
One characteristic of the decoration at Villa di Cetinale is its elegant understatement. Discreet, pale-colored grotesques are the only wall decorations in the corridor.

Below:
The portrait shows Giulio Ranuccio Bianchi Bandinelli and his children. The Napoleonic prefect of the Ombrone department, and later governor of Siena, Giulio bequeathed the property to his son Mario.

Facing:
The bottom edge of the study's vaulted ceiling is decorated with a band of monochrome *putti* and garlands, separated by slim pilasters and the family crest. On the left, next to the fireplace, is a bust of Giulio Ranuccio Bianchi Bandinelli.

Left:
Villa Bianchi Bandinelli has always been a private residence and has thus conserved the spaces and functions of a family house. Shown here, the lovely kitchen and its ancient stone sink.

Below:
The library, another of the villa's charming living spaces, is emblematic of the Bianchi Bandinelli's unswerving devotion to culture and the arts.

courageously decided to cede to his tenant farmers much of the property he had inherited, and also helped them form a cooperative to vinify Chianti. Conscious of the extraordinary historic and artistic value of the villa, Ranuccio Bianchi Bandinelli was keen to conserve its heritage intact. Like a sleeping beauty, attended with immense love and dedication by its owners, Geggiano has managed to preserve undiminished its magical charm.

When Bernardo Bertolucci shot here in 1996 some of the most significant, dream-like scenes from *Stealing Beauty*, people who had never seen the villa were suddenly fascinated by a charm that has survived untarnished, suspended apart from time's chaotic onward rush.

tasks within opulent rocaille borders on the walls of the *Salotto Verde*, or Green Room, on the second floor.

In 1824, the property was left by Giulio Ranuccio Bianchi Bandinelli, the Napoleonic first prefect of the department of Ombrone and then governor of Siena, to his son Mario, who decided not to make any major alterations. His partner in the enterprise was Siena-born Agostino Fantastici, an enormously talented neoclassical architect. This withdrawn but very well-informed Italian Schinkel combined neoclassical grace with elements of Egyptian and neo-Gothic revival. Fantastici's talents were wasted in a city dominated by the ghosts of former glory and a now-dulled ancient splendor. He created some splendid furnishings, as well as the Villa del Pavone (Peacock Villa), conceived between 1825 and 1835. Fantastici's intervention at the Villa del Pavone was the high point of a movement that strove to recover the ancient tradition in an academic mode without, however, restricting itself to the Roman heritage. Instead, he also sought inspiration from the Etruscans and Egyptians for this building, designed for Mario Bianchi Bandinelli, who preferred a less high-profile, more secluded, edifice to the proud *palazzo* his father Giulio had built at Porta Romana. The son rejected pomp and circumstance for the new ideals of the Romantic aesthetic. After several passages across the generations, Mario's Geggiano came down to its present owners, descendants of the celebrated archeologist Ranuccio Bianchi Bandinelli, who passed away in 1976. A leading intellectual and very receptive of the new social ideas, Ranuccio

Medici Villas
Tuscany

Below left:
Michelangiolo Cinganelli's late Mannerist frescoes on the ceiling of the corner loggia at the Medici villa of Careggi flaunt feigned pergolas, allegories, village scenes, and grotesques. The work dates from 1618.

Below:
The porticoed courtyard was probably designed by Michelozzo. Ransacked when the Medicis were driven out of Florence for the second time in 1527, Careggi was sold in 1779 by Grand Duke Pietro Leopoldo of Lorraine to Vincenzo di Donato Orsi, who in 1848 ceded it to Francis Joseph Sloane.

The origins of the Medicis are obscure, but we know that in the Middle Ages, the family moved from the countryside at Mugello to Florence. The steps in their ineluctable ascent of the city's economic and political ladder were marked by the purchase or construction of villas. The Medicis expanded first into the area north of Florence, then into Valdarno. Cosimo the Elder, the real founder of the Medici fortune, owned Cafaggiolo and Trebbio. Built almost as castles, these homes reveal the importance the family attached to farming. The layout of their quiet, unassuming gardens anticipates the new humanistic culture. They are reassuring residences, far from the tumult and crowds of late medieval city life.

Cafaggiolo and Trebbio are dedicated to the cultural *otia* and the achievement of natural harmony in country life that was so dear to the poet Horace, and reconstructed by the humanists on the ruins of classical antiquity. A Tuscan country estate is the setting for Giovanni Boccaccio's *Decameron*. In it, a group of gallant young sophisticates from the professional and merchant nobility flees from the terrible Black Death that ravaged Florence in 1348, taking shelter in the comfortable isolation of an out-of-town villa. We can already see its new architecture, opening timidly to meld into the surrounding landscape and the bucolic rhythms of agricultural tasks. One of the few structures that always graced the light-filled spaces of the garden was the rustic pergola, of classical origin, resting on slim brick columns. The early Renaissance garden was a place of shelter and peace, invigorated by a perfect, even abstract, spatial clarity and permeated by mathematically precise lighting. We see this at Villa Careggi, much loved by Piero the Gouty and his son, Lorenzo the Magnificent, who died there at the age of just over forty on April 8, 1492.

Today, the villa is suffocated by the disorderly advance of urban development, and Florence's hospital complex looms near, but until relatively recently, it nestled among gentle hills and lush fields. The Renaissance villa, laid out on a single long axis, was the villa of Man, firmly ensconced at the center of the universe. It was the *hortus*, or garden, where the classical heritage blended harmoniously with the Christian tradition.

The villa of San Pietro at Careggi, which the Medicis acquired from Tommaso Lippi in 1417, differs from the older castle-style residences more in terms of its function than in practical detail. Shortly afterwards, between 1437 and 1456, the Medicis purchased eleven neighboring farms and a further twenty-seven properties figure in the *portate al catasto* (land registry reports) for 1480. Lying not far from Florence, Careggi was used as an alternative residence for short stays or major official events. It was also a retreat and a place of convalescence. In 1439, the banquet in honor of Francesco Sforza was held at Careggi and it was here that Lorenzo the Magnificent chose to spend the final days of his life.

Restructuring, to plans by Cosimo the Elder's favorite architect, Michelozzo, went on from the 1440s to the 1460s. The frontage looking onto the garden is symmetrical with respect to the main entrance and its Renaissance spirit is much more obvious than that of the massive, "castellated" front on the road, crowned by a crenellated dwarf gallery projecting on brackets and arches. Unlike the Medici villas at Mugello, Careggi presents a stylistic cross-fertilization of diverse elements. Only Michelozzo could have juxtaposed octagonal columns with classical in the very limited space of a courtyard. We are very far from the ambitious, regular manner, at once innovative and ancient, employed by the architect in the other great private Medici commission, the Florentine *palazzo* in Via

Right:
The south facade of Villa di Careggi, showing the exterior of the corner loggia on the second floor. Restraint and sobriety are the keynotes of an architecture that strives to create the appropriate atmosphere for the intellectual pursuits and learned conversations dear to Humanism.

Below:
The main facade of the Medici villa at Poggio a Caiano. The two "pincer" staircases designed by Pasquale Poccianti were originally intended to run parallel to each other and perpendicular to the facade.

Larga, now known as Palazzo Medici-Riccardi. The villa is traditional, modest, sober, and designed for intellectual pursuits or learned conversations with humanist friends involved in the Certame Coronario poetry competition. Lorenzo's circle included noted intellectuals of the day such as Leon Battista Alberti, Pico Della Mirandola, Poliziano, Cristoforo Landino, Filippo Valori, Donatello, and Carlo Marsuppini, as well as the young and impulsive Michelangelo. In effect, Careggi was built to rival the tranquil country residences described by Petrarch at Vaucluse and Arquà, in the Colli Euganei hills. The *palazzo* and the villa became eloquent emblems for the two

facets of Medici policy in the mid fifteenth century. On the one hand, the Medicis liked to exercise their influence from behind the scenes, maneuvering the merry-go-round of Florence's public offices through loyal intermediaries. However, we should not forget their high-profile patronage of public and religious works, or Benozzo Gozzoli's fresco of the *Journey of the Magi* in the chapel of their Florentine *palazzo*. Such patronage was intended to proclaim the true extent of the family's far-reaching power. Cosimo the Elder's straightforward expectations were expressed in a letter to his friend, the Neoplatonic philosopher, Marsilio Ficino.

Ransacked when the Medicis were driven out of Florence for the second time in 1527, Careggi was sold in 1779 by Grand Duke Pietro Leopoldo of Lorraine

to Vincenzo di Donato Orsi, who in 1848 ceded it to Francis Joseph Sloane.

Poggio a Caiano is a further step along the road to absolute grandeur. The residence was designed to convey the Medicis' obvious dynastic ambitions and attract the admiration of the world at large. It stands on a spur of Monte Ginestra, on land that had belonged to the ancient Cancellieri family from Pistoia, and then to Giovanni Rucellai. Designed by Lorenzo the Magnificent himself, with Giuliano da Sangallo, and begun around 1480, it was originally a large white structure on a rustic base that recalls Leon Battista Alberti's plan a few years earlier for the Gonzaga church of San Sebastiano at Mantua. There are two semicircular flights of stairs leading from the first floor to the terrace and the raised entrance. The stairs were erected by Giuseppe Cacialli to plans from 1807 by Pasquale Poccianti. Originally, they lay parallel to each other and perpendicular to the facade. The portico set into the main facade resembles a classical temple, standing out as a purely symbolic element with its Della Robbia terracotta frieze, the white figures on their blue background surmounted by the proud Medici coat of arms. The probable author of the portico is Andrea Sansovino. The glorious Medici epic was now at its apogee, flaunting a regal pride by selecting and reinterpreting archeological details from classical antiquity.

Building work was interrupted by Lorenzo's death before the completion of the vault of the central hall, which features coffering and terracotta white and gold tiles bearing the family's arms, crests, and emblems. A popular revolt drove the

Preceding pages:
Fresco by Alessandro Allori in the *Salone di Leone X* at Poggio a Caiano. The work celebrates the mission of Lorenzo the Magnificent to Naples in 1479, which ended with the signing of an important peace treaty. The fresco shows Scipio dining with Syphax, king of Numidia.

Facing:
Details of the frescoed flowers, leaves, and *putti* in the *Sala da Biliardo* (Billiard Room), completed in the nineteenth century by Gaetano Lodi at the Medici villa of Poggio a Caiano during restoration under the Savoys.

Left:
Another allegorical fresco in the *Salone di Leone X*, depicting. *The Consul Flaminius Addressing the Council of the Achaean League*, a subject clearly inspired by Lorenzo the Magnificent's speech to the Diet of Cremona. The work is by Alessandro Allori.

Below:
The fresco of the *Triumph of Caesar* alludes to the wondrous gifts sent to Lorenzo by the sultan of Egypt. The work, again in the *Salone di Leone X*, was completed by Andrea del Sarto between 1578 and 1582.

1530 of the imperial army, and the subsequent bloody repression of the revolt by the second Medici pope, Clement VII, foreshadowing the definitive installation of the family on the throne of Tuscany. The scandal-haunted, autocratic, unbalanced Alessandro, last in the male line of the family's main branch, was to be assassinated in 1537 by his cousin Lorenzino. Then in 1569, Pius V ratified the family's grand-ducal rank and, at last, the star of Cosimo I was in the ascendant. Cosimo came from the cadet branch of the family, but through his mother, Maria Salviati, herself the daughter of a Medici, the blood of the family's glorious forebears ran in his veins. However, let us get back to our story. From 1519 to 1521, Andrea del Sarto and Franciabigio worked side by side at Poggio a Caiano in the main hall, with its richly decorated gilt coffered ceiling. Del Sarto created two frescoes of the *Triumph of Caesar*, which according to the iconographic scheme drawn up by Paolo Giovio, commemorated the gifts sent by the Sultan of Egypt to Lorenzo the Magnificent, while Franciabigio painted the *Return of Cicero,* evoking the triumphal return to Florence of the *pater patriae,* Cosimo the Elder, in 1434. At the same time, the tormented genius, Pontormo, was painting the marvelous lunette with *Vertumnus and Pomona,* which was to attract widespread attention and become a benchmark for the resurgent Arcadian movement. From 1578 to 1582, the commission to complete the hall, known as the *Salone di Leone X,* was given to Alessandro Allori.

Medicis from Florence in November 1494, but they returned in 1498. In 1513, one of Lorenzo's sons, Cardinal Giovanni Medici, was elected to the papacy and took the name Leo X, an event that confirmed the international status of the family from Mugello. After the dispersal of the last followers of Girolamo Savonarola, the reformist Dominican friar and scourge of ecclesiastical and political corruption who was burnt at the stake in Piazza della Signoria on May 23, 1498, it was Leo X who enthusiastically recommenced building work at Poggio a Caiano, a villa that was so intimately bound up with the legend of his father, Lorenzo the Magnificent. The Medicis, in the persons of Ippolito and Alessandro, were expelled for a second time in a vain attempt by the Florentines to restore the republican regime. Despite innumerable acts of heroism, the ensuing siege ended with the entry into Florence on August 12,

In the seventeenth century, Anton Domenico Gabbiani, Crown Prince Ferdinando's favorite artist, added stuccoes. The villa was already famous in the fifteenth century, from the description by Agnolo Poliziano in his *Ambra*, and in the baroque period, it was the place of confinement for Marguerite Louise d'Orleans, the depressive, neurotic wife of Cosimo III. New construction work was carried out under the Lorraines, including the theater, which dates from 1772. During the reign of Elisa Baciocchi in the early nineteenth-century Napoleonic period, various other buildings and decorative interventions were completed. Finally, in the decade from 1860 to 1870,

Poggio a Caiano became the residence of Vittorio Emanuele II of Savoy and his second, morganatic wife, the shapely Bela Rusin. Born Rosa Vercellana, she was the daughter of a drummer in the Savoy army who, thanks to her long affair with the sovereign, became Countess of Mirafiori. After 1865, more work on the furnishings and interior decoration, for example in the billiard room, was carried out under the direction of the architect, Antonio Sajler. During his stays at the villa, Vittorio Emanuele dedicated much of his time to his favorite pastime, hunting, just as the Medicis has done before him. The Medicis had in fact owned a huge estate that stretched from Poggio a Caiano to

Above:
The second-floor entrance hall at Poggio a Caiano is decorated with monochrome neoclassical wall panels commissioned by Elisa Baciocchi.

Left:
Desfossé wallpaper depicting South American natives in a jungle setting. The subject was chosen by Elisa Baciocchi to decorate a first-floor room at Villa di Poggio a Caiano in the early nineteenth century.

Following pages:
The garden of the Medici Villa di Castello, designed by Benedetto Varchi and laid out by Niccolò Pericoli, known as *Il Tribolo*. On the right is the marvelous central fountain, harmoniously set in a precise geometrical pattern of box hedges.

Left:
An aerial view of the Medici Villa di Castello, today the home of the Accademia della Crusca Italian language institution. The superb Mannerist garden may be admired in all its geometrical perfection.

Below:
The long front elevation of Villa di Castello, facing onto the *piazzale*.

Artimino and the Arno, where they engaged in the hunts immortalized in a series of tapestries known as *The Hunts at Poggio a Caiano*, woven to cartoons by the Flemish artist, Jean van der Straet, or Joannus Stradanus, in 1559.

We shall go back for a moment to the sixteenth century. Times were changing. Dramas were unfolding. Policies, strategies, and alliances were forming and dissolving on the European scene. The fall of Neoplatonism, the crisis

Above and below:
Two bran shovels conserved in the museum at Villa di Castello. They belonged to Gherardo Gherardi and Benedetto Gori, both members of the Accademia della Crusca (literally, the "Academy of Chaff"). The mottoes chosen by the two academicians were "entwined" and "quiet."

Left:
This giant bronze figure (1559) of *Winter* (or *January*) is the work of Ammannati. The statue stands on an artificial islet beyond which begins the *selvatico*, or country scene, of the upper garden.

Facing:
One of the three basins encrusted with fish and shellfish by Ammannati, bearing groups of real and imaginary animals sculpted by Giambologna.

Following pages:
The generously proportioned ballroom at the Medici Villa della Petraia was erected in the days of Vittorio Emanuele II of Savoy. The sixteenth-century inner courtyard was covered with a large iron and glass skylight.

Facing:
A longitudinal view of the *sotto colonnato* (under colonnade). The back wall was frescoed by Volterrano with the *Meeting of Pope Leo X and King Francis I of France*.

Left:
The front elevation of the Medici Villa della Petraia is noteworthy for the balanced sobriety of its decoration.

Below:
The Medici Villa della Petraia is a short distance from the Villa di Castello. It was created, at considerable effort, out of a fortified fourteenth-century residence that passed to the Medici family in 1530.

of Renaissance certainties, the bitter realization that the control over the cosmos to which Humanism aspired had been lost, endless political crises, and threats from foreign armies all conspired to make Nature, with her vibrant, life-bearing sap and her disquietingly undomesticated urges, the absolute protagonist of the garden. In the middle decades of the sixteenth century, the mannerist garden astounded and perturbed the visitor with its mirror-image metaphysical illusions, extravagant interplay of allegories and magic symbols, and endless surprises. The garden also acquired political significance. We need only think of the fountain dominated by the group of sculptures representing *Hercules Suffocating Anteus*, by Bartolomeo Ammannati for Villa di Castello. It clearly alludes to Cosimo's triumph over his enemies. The meeting of various water courses symbolizes the perfect organization of Tuscany's water

system, and the new prosperity deriving from the grand duke's enlightened rule. The villa is eloquent testimony to the shift toward neo-feudalism in Tuscany. The Antica Repubblica had fallen in 1530, when the investiture of the emperor, Charles V, created the duchy, which from 1569 was the grand duchy of Tuscany under the Medici dynasty. Since that time, grand-ducal villas have sprung up all over the Tuscan states to triumphantly advertise the Medicis' absolute power while providing an impressive system of territorial control. As we examine the celebrated lunettes by the Flemish artist, Giusto Utens, whose elegant, almost photographic, virtuosity graces the principal Medici residences, we realize at once how important the villas were in the wide-ranging political strategy pursued by the family, and how the residences served to bolster an image of power that was increasingly wreathed in the gilded splendor of dynastic aspirations.

Castello, to the north of Florence, was originally called Il Vivaio, or the Nursery. It was inherited by Caterina Sforza Riario, a vigorous, warlike Renaissance woman, on the death of her husband, Giovanni de' Medici, Il Popolano (of the people). The cadet branch of the Medici family had acquired it through Giovanni and Lorenzo di Pierfrancesco de' Medici in 1477. Botticelli's masterpieces, the *Birth of Venus* and *Spring*, hung here and it was at Castello that, a few decades later, Pontormo arrived to work on frescoes that have since been lost. Caterina was the mother of the celebrated *condottiero* Giovanni dalle Bande Nere, who spent his childhood here and whose son, Cosimo, duke of Florence from 1537, inherited it. Castello's glory, however, is the garden, laid out to a carefully conceived ideological and allegorical plan by Benedetto Varchi. The material author of the project was Niccolò Pericoli, nicknamed *Il Tribolo*, who created a spectacular show of Mannerist inventions. In the center of the formal grid of box hedges is the fountain of *Hercules*, completed by Ammanati in 1546 at Pericoli's suggestion. On the rampart supporting the great upper basin is a magical grotto, with rockery and stalactites in multicolored stone. The three basins are encrusted with fish, shellfish, and crustaceans carved by Ammannati. Above them is a disquieting group of real and imaginary animals by Giambologna. Dominating the whole is the unicorn,

symbolizing Cosimo I. A final dramatic touch is added by the tormented, grotesque bronze giant representing *Winter*, or *January,* again by Ammannati. He crouches on a hillock over the green water of a basin, behind which begins the *selvatico*, or country scene.

After Cosimo's death, Buontalenti doubled the villa's main building for Francesco I, adding the ashlar doorway, and in the seventeenth century, Cardinal Giovan Carlo de' Medici, an enthusiastic opera lover, assembled a collection of citrus fruit in large vases of Impruneta terracotta. Six hundred species are still conserved at the villa. The oranges, bergamots, citrons, aromatic lemons, hybrids, and rarities also fascinated the Lorraines, who succeeded the Medicis on the throne of Tuscany. Castello passed to the house of Savoy when Florence became capital of Italy in 1860, and in 1919, it was donated by Vittorio Emanuele III to the republic of Italy. Today, it is the home of the Accademia della Crusca, Italy's language institute.

La Petraia stands not far from Castello. It is a converted fourteenth-century fortified farmhouse that belonged to the Brunelleschi family. In 1422, it was acquired by Palla Strozzi and, in 1468, by Benedetto Salutati. Having passed to the Medicis in 1530, this *casa da signore*, or gentleman's house, as it was referred to until 1566, was given two years later by Cosimo I to his son Ferdinando. On becoming grand duke, Cardinal Ferdinando de' Medici may have

entrusted building work to Bernardo Buontalenti. Ferdinando liked to spend the summer at La Petraia with his wife, Cristina of Lorraine. At the villa, the memory of the Medicis is constantly interwoven with that of the Lorraines, and then of the Savoys. The house of Savoy took possession of La Petraia in 1859, when it became the official residence of the countess of Mirafiori. In the reception rooms and in the private apartments of the king and his morganatic wife, we find frescoes by Poccetti, as well as large gilt mirrors, Louis Quinze and Empire decorations, eclectic mid nineteenth-century furniture, sumptuous Genoese velvet drapes, Renaissance tables, and eighteenth-century tapestries or sixteenth-century Medici tapestries. Highlights include *Bathsheba at her Bath*, a Medici tapestry completed in the seventeenth century. The opulent, composite decor is in the nineteenth-century idiom. The pretentiously academic official entertaining style of the new Kingdom of

Above left:
The upper loggia of the covered court at Villa della Petraia is frescoed with bucolic landscapes.

Above:
This detail of the *Studio di Vittorio Emanuele II* at the Medici Villa della Petraia reveals the eclectic nature of the lavish furnishings commissioned by the Savoys.

Facing above:
Detail of the loggia at Villa di Artimino featuring the scenographic three-flight staircase, completed in 1930 by the architect Enrico Lusini.

Facing right:
The west-facing facade of the Medici Villa di Artimino is often mistaken for the front elevation because of the great staircase that is a twentieth-century addition.

Italy jostles with the layered accumulations of an illustrious, if awkward, past and the new requirements of the bourgeoisie, such as comfort and the historicist decorative schemes beloved of mid nineteenth-century taste. In the huge Italian garden designed by Tribolo, the elaborately elegant central marble *Fiorenza* fountain is adorned with *Venus Anadyomene*, a bronze copy of Hellenistic grace specially cast by Giambologna for La Petraia to represent Florence as the goddess of love. This ensemble introduces a broad, three-level terrace. In front is a fishpond, over which rises the low, simplified, two-story edifice, its frontage dominated by a square embattled tower. This is a sort of belvedere, floating in the clear Tuscan air and offering a splendid, all-round view over the marshy flatlands, the capital, the valley of the river Arno, and the hill slopes dotted with villas, farmhouses, cypresses, and crops that rise toward Monte Morello.

In the nineteenth century, the garden was made over in the romantic style by the Bohemian garden designer, Joseph Frietsch, who was commissioned by the Lorraines. To the rear, is the luxuriant park with its fishponds. The sixteenth-century courtyard is set within the main building and surrounded by elaborate seventeenth-century frescoes by

Baldassarre Franceschini, called *Il Volterrano*, exalting the glory of the Medicis and the exploits of the *Cavalieri di Santo Stefano* (Knights of Saint Stephen). The courtyard was covered with a glass skylight to convert it into a ballroom for Vittorio Emanuele II. Artimino, a plain, austere villa not far from Prato, was also designed by Bernardo Buontalenti, Francesco I de' Medici's architect. Francesco succeeded his father, Cosimo I, in 1576. The threesome, made up of the grand duke, his controversial second wife Bianca Cappello (Francesco's scandalously flaunted mistress), and Buontalenti, gave rise to a wealth of ambitious artistic and architectural projects, choreographies, fairy-tale theatrical spectacles, secular and religious ceremonies, experiments that mingled science with alchemy and necromancy, and eye-catching buildings designed in the language of the "marvelous." The villa at Artimino is also called *Ferdinanda*, after Grand Duke Ferdinando, the brother and heir of Francesco I. He succeeded to the title after his brother's sudden and mysterious demise on October 19, 1587, officially from tertian fever. Francesco's demise was followed a few hours later on October 20, by the death of his consort at Poggio a Caiano.

Ferdinando had the villa built, between 1594 and 1600, in the middle of an extensive *barco*, or hunting estate, and it takes the form of a late reinterpretation of the humanism-inspired fortress-villa. Artimino features four stout escarped ramparts, one at each corner, and its function as a hunting lodge is the reason for the simplicity of its structure and decoration, which uses only a few, concise, ornamental motifs. The building presents a compact, geometric volume. The center of the west-facing front is enlivened by a five-span architraved loggia and three large windows opening onto a balcony on the main facade. An air of extreme severity is contrasted only by the jungle of bizarre chimneys that rise over the roof, an imaginative hint at the older style adopted by the young architect in the days of Francesco I. Times had changed, as Buontalenti was very much aware.

Buontalenti's complex architectural language was leaner, simpler, and more abstract. We should remember that this was at the height of the Counter-Reformation and the grand duke himself had once been a cardinal. We should also bear in mind the new direction taken by the Medicis and the vigorous restoration of feudalism that was under way. Nor could a garden, the centerpiece of any mannerist villa, be allowed to disturb the squat, castle-like mass of Artimino, since the hill suffers from a chronic lack of water. In 1930, the architect Enrico Lusini built the three spectacular flights of steps, two of which are curved, basing them on an architectural drawing attributed to Bernardo Buontalenti. As a result, the villa's internal layout is much simplified. Two reception rooms face each other across the entrance hall, leading to adjacent communicating side rooms. One of these is the so-called *Salone Pubblico*, or Public Room, otherwise known as the *Salone delle Ville* (Room of the Villas) because it was decorated a series of lunettes by Giusto Utens that document,

with impressively photographic precision and an almost surreal wealth of detail, the various Medici estates. There is an especially wide and varied range of painted decoration. In the *loggia dei Paradisi*, we find the grand-ducal crest, the famous Medici balls. According to some authorities, these are actually pills, alluding to the profession of apothecary thought to have been practiced by the Medicis' forebears before the family's rise to power. Other decoration includes stucco chains and garlands, as well as paintings and ovals with elaborate frames, but pride of place goes to the dazzling

allegorical portraits by Domenico Passignano of *Poetry*, *History*, *Solicitude*, *Diligence*, *Weariness*, and *Patience*. After a brief interruption for the religious decoration of the chapel, the allegorical theme continues in Fernando's rooms, adopting themes suitable for a warrior monarch, such as *Heroic Virtue*. In contrast, *Obedience*, *Chastity*, and *Fidelity*, the wifely virtues indispensable to a prolific, successful matrimonial union, were the symbols chosen to watch as tutelary spirits over Grand Duchess Cristina of Lorraine.

Facing above:
The allegory of *Felicity*, painted by Domenico Passignano in the vault of the main reception hall at Villa di Artimino.

Facing left:
Domenico Passignano painted the *Banquet of Octavian and Livia* in the center of the ceiling vault in the main reception hall.

Right:
A nocturnal view of the *Loggia dei Paradisi* showing the impressive grand-ducal crests, frescoed chains and garlands, and the *Allegories* painted by Domenico Passignano.

VILLA DI SAMMEZZANO
FLORENCE, TUSCANY

On some clear winter nights, when it is suffused in the moon's chill light, even travelers speeding along the Autostrada del Sole on the flatland below can see the elongated lines of the Villa di Sammezzano standing out distinctly against the backdrop of the austere Valdarno hills. Massive, assured, and indifferent to the passage of the centuries, it dominates the sweeping countryside that surrounds it. Some of the moldings and the brickwork battlements ennobling the front, the ornate stonework around the windows, and, especially, the Mogul-style central tower may suggest to closer observers the decorative motif of the interior. However, it is difficult to imagine the ambition, the scope, the microcosm of make-believe, and the astonishing eccentricity of the reinterpreted Moorish repertoire that comes magically to life in the rooms inside.

Villa di Sammezzano is an Alhambra that has, magically, been made to appear in the heart of Tuscany, in the wild, open hills of Valdarno that Piero della Francesca and Leonardo da Vinci loved so dearly in the feverishly creative days of the Renaissance. The dream took physical shape in stone, not because of a spell cast by some Arabian Nights genie of the lamp but because it was conceived and created in the mid-nineteenth century by the nobleman who owned the property. Marquis Ferdinando Panciatichi acquired the castle with its extensive grounds and woods in 1816, on the death of his maternal aunt, Ferdinando Ximenes

Facing:
The multi-colored *Sala dei Gigli* (Lily Room) owes its name to the many red heraldic fleur-de-lis of Aragon set on the shafts of the dark blue columns supporting the ceiling, made up of pointed arches decorated with ribbing.

This page:
The *Sala dei Pavoni* (Peacock Room) re-interprets the style and decorative techniques of the Alhambra, with the clear intention of remaining as faithful as possible to the original model.

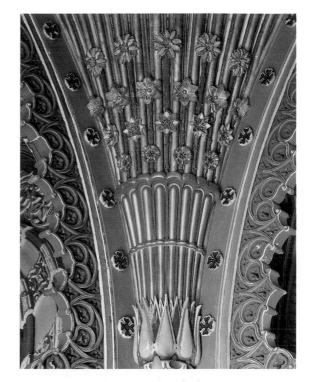

d'Aragona, brother of his mother Vittoria and the last scion of a noble Spanish house that had enjoyed great fortune in the Grand Duchy of Tuscany since the sixteenth century. Owned in ancient times by the noble Florentine Altoviti family, and then enfeoffed by the Grand Duke, Cosimo I, to the Marquis of Marignano, Giovan Jacopo de' Medici, Sammezzano with its vast estate "in the community of San Salvatore al Leccio," between Rignano sull'Arno and Incisa, was ceded by the marquis in the latter half of the sixteenth century to Sebastiano Ximenes, a senator and Signore of Saturnia, who established his family's first foothold in Tuscany. The noble Ximenes family, closely connected to the Medici court, was also entitled to use the prestigious predicate "d'Aragona." *Fiero Sangue d'Aragona, Scorre nelle Mie Vene* (Proud Blood of Aragon Courses in My Veins), wrote the marquis on the walls of his country residence, where letters of gold also traced Latin mottoes such as

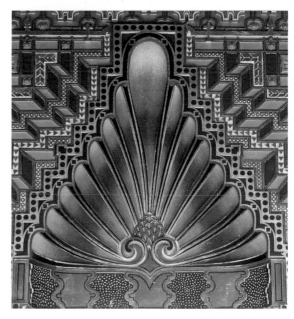

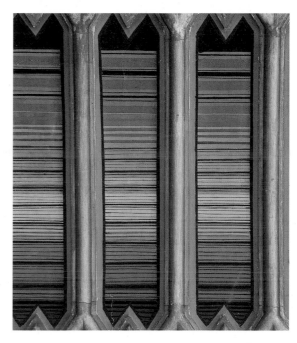

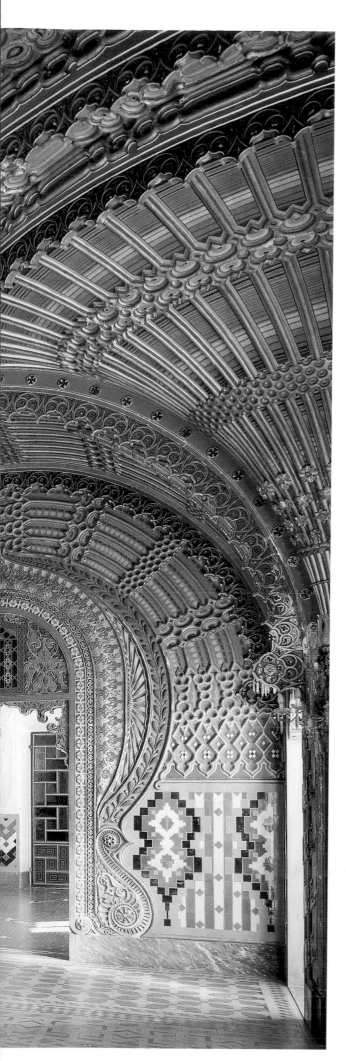

Following pages counterclockwise from upper left:
The loggia and balcony of the *Sala Bianca* (White Room). The highly unusual dome is covered with a complex pattern of white stucco.

The *Sala degli Amanti* (Lovers' Room) evokes the medieval literary theme of the chivalrous romance and its heroes.

The main entrance hall, on two floors, has a gallery and open-work balustrade, a multi-colored lacunar ceiling, and papyrus-capital paired columns.

Facing:
The stupendous *Sala dei Pavoni* is decorated with translucent ceramic tiles and geometric shapes in majolica.

Below:
The *Sala dei Piatti Spagnoli*, or Room of the Spanish Plates, takes its name from the dozens of enameled plates from the Iberian peninsula set into its ribbed ceiling.

Solve Nodum (Loose the Knot) and *Non Plus Ultra* (The Best of All).

But let us return to our story. Finally, the villa passed to Marquis Ferdinando Panciatichi, who inherited the estate and titles of his namesake and also assumed, with the consent of his father Niccolò, his surname and noble predicates after a long and exasperating legal wrangle. Work began in 1853 and was to continue for more than forty years. To transform the simple original building into the fabulous Moorish palace of his dreams, Ferdinando Panciatichi drew inspiration from the travel books and tourist guides, from Great Britain in particular, that were circulating around Europe at the time. The most famous of these was the Baedeker guide that

NON PLUS

Above:
The entrance hall on the ground floor is dominated by the Latin motto, *Non Plus Ultra* (The Best of All), whose colors change as the day progresses, thanks to light from the large multi-colored windows on the floor above.

Right:
The small chapel at Villa di Sammezzano is also decorated in the Moorish style.

unfailingly accompanied the restless protagonists of the novels of Foster, Edith Wharton, and Henry James on the burgeoning tourist circuit. Panciatichi may, of course, have gone straight to the fountainhead and purchased the two volumes, published by Owen Jones in 1842 and 1843, that revealed to a wider international readership the marvelous ornamentation in the palace and gardens of the Moorish kings of Granada. The book was certainly available to, and appreciated by, the numerous members of the cultured and eccentric British colony that installed itself in the Florence of the Lorraines during the early nineteenth century.

The unifying Moorish theme at Sammezzano did not undergo any dramatically scenic transformations, or free invention in a historicist vein. It had nothing at all to do with the delicious contamination pastiches and pictorial reinterpretations that breathe life into so many *turqueries*, the exotic style of decoration from high eighteenth-century rocaille, comparable to the chinoiseries that found fertile terrain and endless applications in the controversial early decades of the nineteenth century.

One after the other, the interiors of the Castello di Sammezzano open like sets on a stage to tell a story that offers an overview of the Alhambra's stylistic and technical repertoire. There is a clear desire to adhere to and be faithful to the original model. One exception is the *Sala degli Amanti* (Lovers' Room), which evokes the medieval literary tradition of chivalrous romance and its heroes, Tristan and Isolde, Lancelot and Guinevere, Tancredi and Clorinda, and the crusading knights and defenders of western Christendom. It is no coincidence that these are in the "west" wing of the building.

The interiors created by Ferdinando Panciatichi for his country residence explode with almost cinematographic impact in the dominant ornamentation of the Moorish decorative key. Seductive Byzantine and Gothic motifs, the sensuality of a Persian garden, *retour d'Egypte* papyrus columns, verses from the Bible and Koran on the intrados of the arches, stars of David, kaleidoscopic points of view that direct the gaze to lavish backdrops, fragments of mirrors, mystic maxims from the Sufi tradition, gold leaf, and carpets with eye-deceiving patterns all find a place in the home of a man who was lost in an all-consuming obsession. Panciatichi, abandoned by his wife before the forty-year-long building project was complete, used to claim that "all great men come close to madness."

The sumptuous *Sala dei Pavoni* (Peacock Room), is lavishly and colorfully decorated with translucent ceramic tiles and geometric shapes in majolica. These are veined with delicate, complex oriental patterns that intertwine across the floors and walls to continue into the stuccoes on the ceiling. The panels of the *mihrab* doors, set in concentric indented cornices, are decorated with abstract plant motifs on gold leaf.

part of a table service given by the emperor, Charles V, to a member of the family. Here, different materials and techniques converge. Marble inlays rub shoulders with stucco, ceramics, and colored glass, as well as wooden elements and engravings. Cotton-candy white, the *Sala da Ballo* (Ballroom) is decorated with continuous Mozarabic floral designs that extend their sophisticated tendrils above the paneling. Here, the ubiquitous Islamic theme joins with the fifteenth-century Spain of the Reconquista, which emerges in agile floral *pateras*, superimposed stylized urns and palmettes, and in the indented supports of the equally elaborate churrigueresque canopies.

Finally, there is the huge, lavish, main ballroom, which stands in what was once the castle's inner courtyard. A monument to *horror vacui*, or the compulsive decoration of empty space, it is

disposed on two floors and features a gallery with an openwork balustrade, a multi-colored lacunar ceiling, and robust Egyptian-style paired columns. Its interior is illuminated by the ever-changing light that filters through the modulating colors of the large windows. The bathroom is another highlight, with its sarcophagus tub in Carrara marble. Perhaps Sammezzano should be viewed as a single, elaborate allegory, a tribute to the Iberian roots of a family whose male line was extinct, and which had found new life and energy in Vittoria Ximenes' heir. Dream-like aspirations, a proud historic heritage, and a certain megalomaniac eccentricity are all per-ceptible in these rooms, whose unifying decorative scheme is unbroken. The only exception is the bedroom used by the marquis during his frequent, extended stays in Valdarno. Surprisingly, it is bereft of decoration of any sort. Who knows why?

Above and right:
Detail of white stucco decorations in another part of the house. The room on the right provides further evidence of the tenacity with which Marquis Panciatichi pursued his life's architectural dream.

The *Sala dei Gigli* (Lily Room) is also adorned with brightly colored ceramics, stuccoes, and glass. The room takes its name from the red fleur-de-lis of the house of Aragon decorating the dark blue shafts of the columns that bear an intricate medley of ribbed pointed arches. Then come the *Sala del Giuramento* (Room of the Oath), and the impressive *Sala delle Stalattiti* (Stalactite Room). The *Sala dei Piatti Spagnoli* (Room of the Spanish Plates) takes its name from the dozens of enameled plates set into the ceiling. According to tradition, they were

199

PALAZZO MATTEI-CAETANI DI SERMONETA

ROME, LAZIO

Throughout the long history of papal Rome, political and social prestige was asserted in the magnificence of the city's residences, the ambition of their architectural concepts, and the decoration of their exteriors, whether the patrons were princes of the Church or members of the lay nobility. Sumptuous *palazzi* transformed the streets and *piazze* into theatrical sets, advertising the economic power and social status of their owners. In the nineteenth century, Hippolyte Taine said of Rome's aristocratic residences, "you can get a shrewd idea of the animal from its shell." The historic center of modern Rome boasts many such buildings with centuries-long heritages of influence, art, and ostentation. Frequently, these magnificent homes have been converted into offices, courts, or museums open to the public, as is the case with Villa Borghese, ceded to the state by the Borghese family in the early twentieth century. Others have also opened their

treasures to the public and one such is Palazzo Doria-Pamphilj, an astonishingly rich gallery of art, still in the hands of the family that created it and protected by a legally binding trust. Yet, there are some *palazzi* in the city that still serve as residences, at once Aladdin's caves of beauty and temples to ancient family traditions.

One of these is Palazzo Caetani, whose simple, austere front in the manner of Sangallo looks onto Via delle Botteghe Oscure. Since 1967, the residence of the ambassador of Brazil to the Holy See, the *palazzo* is situated in Rione Sant'Angelo. This district corresponds to the ninth Augustan region, whose symbol was a fish. Rione Sant'Angelo takes its name from the medieval church of Sant'Angelo in Pescheria, erected in the eighth century in Portico d'Ottavia. Many families arrived in Rome from all over Italy either in the entourage of a newly nominated cardinal, or in search of fortune and lucrative appointments after a relative's election to the papacy. The Mattei, however, were an ancient Roman house. The family ruled this area of the city, turning it into a stronghold as they maneuvered their way through the turbulent ebb and flow of Roman political life. They left a significant mark and created the so-called *isola Mattei*, or Mattei island. The *palazzo*, whose full title is Mattei-Caetani, was built for Alessandro Mattei, who probably started work on it in 1545. Palazzo Mattei already features in Bufalini's plan of Rome, dated 1551. The architect may be identified as Claudio or Annibale Lippi,

sons of another leading figure in sixteenth-century Roman residential architecture, the Tuscan Nanni di Baccio Bigio, who had already been commissioned by the Matteis to build the family's houses on Piazza Mattei. Asdrubale Mattei, Alessandro's son, was to live here during the construction of the adjacent Palazzo Mattei di Giove.

This glorious edifice features a first court and internal loggia studded with reliefs and ancient busts. It remained in the family until 1938, the Matteis having started building in 1598 for Asdrubale's spectacular wedding to Costanza Gonzaga. "He wished to place himself with Asdrubale," noted Giulio Mancini in his biography, describing the early days in Rome of Michelangelo Merisi, now universally known as Caravaggio. Asdrubale Mattei was a Roman noble enrolled in the *Gentilhuomini Amatori*

(Gentlemen Amateurs) who founded the association of artists in Rome, the Accademia di San Luca. He was also the brother of Ciriaco Mattei, one of the leading avant-garde collectors and patrons, who would later pay an enormous sum of money for three of Caravaggio's most celebrated paintings, commissioning a fourth, the *Capture of Christ*. Asdrubale, whose collection included a lost *Saint Sebastian*, probably offered the artist from Lombardy temporary refuge at his father Alessandro's *palazzo*, the present-day Palazzo Caetani, or in the residence he was building next to for himself. He must also have helped Caravaggio financially when, in the subsequent two or three years, the artist "tried to live on his own."

The entrance of Palazzo Mattei-Caetani di Sermoneta takes us into a square courtyard, graced by three series

of arches on each side, the first order Doric, the second Ionic. Beyond this lies a second courtyard with fountains and archeological remains. In 1628, the *palazzo* was sold by the Mattei family to Monsignor Negroni, whose family lived there for about eighty years. In 1761, it passed to Cardinal Serbelloni from Milan and was finally purchased in 1775 by the duke of Sermoneta, Francesco Caetani. The Caetani, or Gaetani, family descend from the *ipati* (dukes) of Gaeta. In the thirteenth century, Loffredo I fathered Loffredo II and Benedetto, who became pope with the name Boniface VIII from 1294 to 1303. A controversial pontiff at a very difficult moment in history, Boniface VIII was roundly condemned by Dante, his sworn political adversary. Boniface organized the first great Jubilee to promote the Eternal City as a destination for pilgrims for the whole of Christendom, before the outrageous attack he suffered at Anagni at the hands of the emissaries of Philippe le Bel. Boniface was not the first pope to come from Caetani stock. Before him, the house had already given the Church Gelasius II, whose secular name was Giovanni Caetani.

Gelasius was elected to the papal throne in 1118 but remained there for just one year. The reception rooms on the second floor of the *palazzo* make up a superb living unit, complete and intact in its original dimensions, decoration, and splendid furnishings. Gilt baroque consoles with marble tops, collections of porcelain from Meissen, Dresden, and the East India Company, tapestries, a magnificent sixteenth-century Florentine walnut table inlaid with hard stones and mother-of-pearl, Chinese *potiches*, classical statues and reliefs, precious damasks and brocades, family portraits, rocaille *girandoles* and Murano chandeliers, Boulle clocks, flamboyant mirrors, and large oriental rugs all combine in a heritage of rare depth and breadth. On the *piano nobile* is a series of comfortably large rooms. The coffered ceilings bear the Mattei arms of azure and argent, a bend or, on a chief of the last, a double-headed eagle displayed sable, crowned. The sequence of paintings threads its way through the various rooms, ranging across centuries, subjects, stories, and styles. Curious details include the *putti* playing contentedly with cardinal's hats, frescoed by the Antwerp-born Flemish artist, Paul Bril, who enjoyed great success in sixteenth- and seventeenth-century Rome, working side by side with Guido Reni on the Casino dell'Aurora and on the loggia of Palazzo Pallavicini Rospigliosi.

Facing:
In the *Sala Luigi XVI*, or Louis XVI Room, hang frescoes by Zuccari illustrating Alexander the Great and Roxana.

Below:
A delicate portrait of Princess Carlotta Ondedei Caetani, the second wife of Michelangelo I Caetani, by Ludovico Mazzanti.

To decorate the chapel, the Matteis commissioned the Tuscan artist, Pomarancio, at about the same time. In the Louis XVI room, which takes its name from the eighteenth-century embroidered silk hangings on the walls, we find Taddeo Zuccari. In the late sixteenth century, Zuccari was one of the most active and important figures of late mannerism and was widely used by the Farnese family for their *palazzo* in Rome and their dynastic "royal apartments" at Caprarola. Zuccari's ceiling frescoes depict historical scenes from the warlike exploits of Alexander the Great. They portray the Macedonian hero receiving the oracle from the priest of Ammon, accepting gifts from Darius' family, and during the crossing of the river Hydaspes. Next, we see the *Defeat of Porus* and finally *Alexander Refusing Water from a Soldier*. The *Wedding of Alexander and Roxana*, again from the brush of Taddeo Zuccari, adorns the ceiling of the *Sala degli Arazzi* (Tapestry Room), its name deriving from its Brussels-woven hangings. These are also dedicated to the legend of Alexander and were woven to cartoons by the Flemish artist, Martin de Vos (1532–1603), a pupil of the "Romanist" Frans Floris, who completed his training in the papal capital and in Venice.

Leandro Fernández de Moratín, the leading eighteenth-century Spanish

writer, noted when he visited Rome in 1794 that members of many aristocratic families "were busy cutting the tails off their horses to make them look English, racing through the entire city in their carriages, noisily cracking their whips, forcing old women to huddle against the walls, insulting immigrants and Jesuits, with supreme insolence and disreputable, criminal faces that you can spot a mile off. . . ." In contrast, the Caetanis as a family were traditionally interested in science and the arts, as well as social matters. In 1778, an astronomical observatory was installed in a loggia on top of the palazzo. Abbot Luigi de Cesaris was appointed the first director. In the latter half of the nineteenth century, Don Leone Caetani, a celebrated scholar of Islam who donated his marvelous library to the Accademia dei Lincei, held erudite lectures on the upper floors of the building. Michelangelo Caetani was a

highly competent artist who created, among other works, a lovely carved table that is still in his family home. He appears with his siblings and father, Prince Onorato, during a hunt in a late nineteenth-century photograph found in the building's archives by Sandra Cattan Naslausky, the penultimate ambassador to live here.

Around 1920, Prince Gelasio Caetani, a skilled hydraulic engineer, decided to drain the Ninfa estate, which had been acquired by Boniface VIII in

1298. Located on the edge of the Pontine marshes, the estate had for centuries been abandoned to malaria. Gelasio also decided to rebuild the ruins of the castle where his forebear, Francesco, had in the early seventeenth century hidden his much prized and very valuable collection of Dutch tulips. This was the origin of the superb Ninfa garden that was constantly and lovingly enlarged by Gelasio's siblings, Roffredo and Leila, with expert assistance from Leila's husband, Hubert Howard. Leila, who died in 1977, was the last of the Caetani line. The mosaic floors in the gallery, like those in the studio, come from Hadrian's Villa at Tivoli, the residence of the philosopher emperor in the second century after Christ. The late eighteenth-century grotesques and tempera landscapes in the extravagant yet graceful dining room are the work of Christoph Unterbergher, or that prophet of the burgeoning neoclassical movement, Anton Raphael Mengs. However, the decoration also reveals the hand of another underrated eighteenth-century artist, Antonio Cavallucci, born at Sermoneta, the Caetanis' main feudal estate, then discovered and protected by Duke Francesco Caetani.

VILLA BORGHESE
ROME, LAZIO

Paul V, whose given name was Camillo Borghese, was a Hispanophile bureaucrat who became pope in 1605. He and his nephew, Cardinal Scipione Caffarelli Borghese, spent immense sums building *palazzi*, churches, and chapels, and in assembling collections of paintings, which required the attention of an army of courtiers and dignitaries. During Paul V's pontificate, the façade of Saint Peter's was completed. A wealth of decoration and ornament was lavished on the Borghese chapel at Santa Maria Maggiore, and at the Quirinale. The redecoration campaign quickly spread to the family's villas on the

Pincio hill and at Frascati. Scipione Borghese was not yet thirty when his uncle acceded to the papal throne. The son of one of Paul V's sisters, he is utterly emblematic of this extraordinary moment in history, and in the history of art. Quick-thinking, lucid, and talented, Scipione was adept at seizing opportunities. His outgoing, cheerful character could be ruthless when gratifying his insatiable lust for ancient

and contemporary art. It was an attitude he shared with Isabella d'Este, Vincenzo I Gonzaga, and Catherine the Great of Russia. Four years after his uncle's election, Scipione had an income of 100,000 *scudos* as he consolidated his family's wealth, doubling that enormous figure in the final years of Paul V's papacy.

This colossal fortune enabled him to lay the foundations of the Borghese family's power, purchasing principates, feudal states, and eighty farms around Rome, and above all satisfying his appetite for art. Cardinal Scipione acquired 105 paintings, including various canvases by Caravaggio, of whose work he was a particularly avid collector. There were also works that Scipione was able to get his hands on only later, after the collection of the *Cavalier d'Arpino*, Giuseppe Cesari, was confiscated. This unfortunate painter, who was in difficulty with his tax payments, drew no comfort or advantage from being one of the artists to whom the cardinal most frequently gave commissions. As Scipione's power and influence increased exponentially, his obsessive urge to own artworks and possess beauty continued to rage. Raphael's celebrated *Descent from the Cross*, unfortunately embroiled in a bloody Renaissance feud, was daringly removed under cover of darkness from the Baglioni chapel in Perugia, an exploit that caused a popular uprising. The masterpiece was added to the treasures already in the possession of the rapacious prelate.

Another of Scipione's victims, in 1617, was Domenichino. The hapless painter was thrown into prison for having ventured to respect the contract he had stipulated with Cardinal Aldobrandini, who had commissioned from him a *Diana* that Borghese dearly coveted. One way or another, Scipione the "cardinal and nephew" managed to assemble one of the most astounding collections of art ever, driven solely by his boundless,

omnivorous, acquisitiveness. Old masters, mannerists, Rubens, Caravaggio, and Bolognese artists of all inclinations are represented superbly in Scipione's vast collections. His villa on the Pincio, "the delight of Rome," stands in the middle of a huge park. Bedecked with niches, inscriptions, and classical sculptures, it became a focus and stage for the most pleasure-bent social milieu that the Eternal City had seen since the glorious days of the Renaissance. This stately property covers 210 acres and has a circumference of less than four miles outside Porta Pinciana. A place of ostentation, hunting, and extravagant receptions, it was also the home of the cardinal's art collections.

The tormented years of the Counter-Reformation, its moral dilemmas, and the subtle yet violent crisis that had threatened the very fabric of the Roman Catholic Church, now seemed very far away. Instead, there was an explosion of religious, political, and ceremonial power in the stunning imagery of the new baroque movement, the ideal language for the triumph of orthodoxy. The new age heralded the arrival of new, gifted creative artists, including Bernini, Borromini, and Pietro da Cortona. Scipione commissioned a constant stream of outstanding works from the finest of these, who had been attracted to Rome by the cardinal's brilliant architectural, artistic, and social "New Deal." Guido

Facing:
Pluto and Proserpine was sculpted between 1619 and 1625 by Gian Lorenzo Bernini. Bernini also sculpted the *Rape of Proserpine*, *David*, and *Apollo and Daphne*.

Below:
The second hall houses a columned sarcophagus, which dates from A.D. 160 and depicts the Labors of Hercules.

Reni was summoned to paint the fresco of Aurora in one of the cardinal's pleasure lodges, on the slopes of the Quirinal hill at the back of the garden. Today, the lodge is known as Palazzo Pallavicini-Rospigliosi.

Thanks to Borghese, Bernini embarked on a long and fortunate artistic career. Scipione ushered in a new era with his lifestyle, his reputation as a connoisseur, and his liberal, wide-ranging patronage of the arts. Villa Borghese is built on what was once a vineyard that had belonged to the family since 1580. In the Pariolo area, it was traditionally referred to as *Vigna Vecchia* (Old Vineyard) and was extended by another six purchased or donated properties from 1606 to 1609. This surface was the basis for Flaminio Ponzio's *casino*, or pleasure lodge, and for Italian gardens with their box hedges and woods. Work went on in the early years of Paul V's pontificate, when the influence of his nephew Scipione on the government of the Papal States was very evident. The residence was to be finished in 1613, when the dying architect was replaced by Vasanzio. Giovanni Vasanzio, as the Flemish architect Jan van Santen was known, would also take charge of the decoration, covering all four sides with forty-three sculptures, most of them ancient, seventy busts, and 144 bas-reliefs.

This exuberant decorative scheme, its *horror vacui* a hymn to classical art, looked onto two flights of stairs leading down to the *piazzale*, which is enclosed by a balustrade once graced with vases and statues. The courtyard to the rear of the building once had a fountain and Italian gardens on either side. In 1608, Borghese acquired the sculptures from Palazzo Ceoli, today's Palazzo Sacchetti, in Via Giulia and in 1609, he added Giovanni Battista Della Porta's collection, which included sculptures that had originally stood in the ancient basilica of Saint Peter. These were given to him by his uncle, the pope, to mark the commencement of work on the facade of the principal place of Christian worship. From 1610 to 1620, extensions were being made to the *casino* as the estate acquired the neighboring terrain that had belonged

to Scipione's brothers and his nephew Marcantonio, as well as four vineyards with a circumference of more than three miles.

When Vasanzio died in 1621, responsibility for the *casino* and its gardens passed to Girolamo Rainaldi, assisted by Giovanni Fontana for the water installations. The first enclosure in thirteen squares is laid out as a long, elm-lined avenue from Via Pinciana, along the courtyard-theater opposite the residence. The two termini were carved by Pietro Bernini, father of Gian Lorenzo. The Fontana Ovale and Fontana Rotonda are surrounded by pines and firs among box trees and short supporting walls. The green texture of the scenery is broken up by two supports for bird nets. The Loggia dei Vini, erected in 1609, served as a natural cooler. The second enclosure, to the east of the *casino*, was planted with laurels set in six squares by a row of tall cypresses. The *Giardino Segreto* (Secret Garden) and the *Giardino dei Melangoli* (Bitter Orange Garden) begin from the two areas near the residence. At the rear court, there was the *Prospettiva*, with the *Fontana del Narciso* (Fountain of Narcissus). Here were large aviaries, as well as a deer park, and another semicircular court-cum-theater enclosed by box hedges.

Finally, there were the laurels and pines of the Bosco Grande, standing among fountains, statues, and sarcophagi. The third enclosure, to the north of the main building, was left in its natural state. It provided the savage element vital to the contrasts beloved of the baroque mind. A vineyard extends over hill, dale, and flat ground, between wild and domestic animals in the Casa del Gallinaro, which would later become the Fortezzuola, a menagerie of ostriches, peacocks, and even lions. There is a huge fishpond, with forty-two plane trees around it. The Casino del Graziano, which now bears only the family's heraldic dragon, was once adorned with relief decorations on the outside. The *casino* passed to the Borghese estate in 1613 and was used to house some of the august prelate's collection of art. On the death of Paul V in 1621, Scipione suffered a sudden reversal of fortune. Abruptly, the cardinal's receptions and antechambers were abandoned as newer, brighter stars attracted the attention of the courtiers, members of the college of cardinals, artists, sycophants, poets, petitioners, and parasites who had enjoyed his hospitality and generosity. Scipione was left on his own, a bitter man in the cold company of

his treasures, silent witnesses to his former power and enthusiasm for the arts. Villa Borghese languished in a gilded limbo until the latter half of the eighteenth century, its gardens lovingly tended by the Borghese family.

In 1793, Prince Marcantonio IV Borghese launched an ambitious program to renovate the interior of his ancestral home by extending the range of themes of the sculptures and statues in the various rooms. The task was assigned to Antonio Asprucci, assisted by his son Mario. The ambiences that emerged from the effort reveal various distinct stylistic influences. The refinement of the frames on the walls still betrays the imprint of

Rocaille but the neoclassical, archeological taste of the stucco cameos and colored marble floors is equally evident. An Egyptian room was created for the Egyptian antiquities. The frescoes of Apollo highlight the peerless virtuosity of Bernini's *Apollo and Daphne* group. Hermaphroditus and Salmacis adorn the ceiling of the room. The exterior was also to undergo alterations. The double flight of stairs was removed and replaced by the single flight we can see today. The park was further extended with a vineyard and a reed bed.

Asprucci was active in the third enclosure, assisted by the British garden artist, Jacob Moore. Results of this wave

of alterations include the false ruin of the temple of Faustina and the two fountains, the Fontana dei Pupazzi and the Fontana dei Cavalli Marini. The focus of the new arrangement was the *Giardin del Lago*, or Lake Garden, an Eden inspired by the art of Poussin and graced by the *Tempio di Esculapio*, the Temple of Esculapius, on the islet and the Piazzale di Siena for the cruel bareback horse races, the *corse dei berberi*, much loved by the Roman aristocracy. The former Casa del Giardiniere dominating the *piazzale* became the Casino dell'Orologio, so named after the four-faced clock on the tower. Archeological remains discovered on the Borghese estate at Pantano were installed here, while a short distance away, the Casino dell'Alboreto dei Gelsi was converted into a chapel dedicated to the Virgin. Nearby is another false ruin, the Temple of Diana. In 1807, Napoleon forced his brother-in-law, Camillo Borghese, the second husband of his sister Pauline, to hand over many of the antiquities at Villa Borghese. These were swiftly transferred to the new section dedicated to classical art at Vivant Denon's Louvre and many were not even paid for. Every single statue and relief on the facade was removed and taken to imperial France, as were many of the superb decorations that adorned the rooms. In return, there arrived Antonio Canova's *Venus Victrix*, a triumphant naked portrait of the beautiful, amoral Princess Pauline, which had caused an enormous scandal in papal Rome when it was put on display in the vestibule of the Cembalo, the Borghese *palazzo* at Ripetta.

One of the most interesting stories about Pauline is related by Mario Praz in *Gusto Neoclassico* (Neoclassical Taste). The probably apocryphal anecdote tells how the tuberculosis-riddled Romantic poet John Keats used to stroll on the Pincio with his fellow sufferer, Lieutenant Isaac Marmaduke Elton of the Royal Engineers, who was residing in Rome for health reasons. The good-looking officer is rumored to have caught the roving eye of the dissolute princess, who made various attempts to seduce him. But that was not the end of the story. "Canova had just finished his celebrated nude statue of Pauline Bonaparte and the three young men, Keats, Elton, and Severn, went to see it. Severn relates that they adjudged it to be in wonderful bad taste and that Keats gave it the unforgettable name, *Arpa Eolia (Aeolian Harp)*." Praz concludes, however, that the incident, which took place in the fall of 1820, is improbable. Canova had completed his

sculpture in 1805 and Prince Camillo, a conventional Catholic who resented the scandal the portrait had aroused, kept the offending work under lock and key. Keats was to die the following February and Pauline followed him five years later.

Villa Borghese's gardens expanded yet further to extend over the entire area skirted by Muro Torto to Porta del Popolo. The immense expanse of green was given a makeover inspired by a broader vision of the landscape and townscape that aimed to link the villa to the public highway. The last step was the purchase of the Bourbon vineyard in 1833. The following year, the architect Luigi Canina completed the tasks he had been assigned in 1825. In an ambitious project, he laid out avenues and created linking bridges, featuring Egyptian propylaea after the manner of Piranesi, and finally graced the grandiose avenue that leads from the Fontana di Esculapio to Piazzale Flaminio with a scenic entrance. In accordance with the prince's wishes, Villa Borghese lost its predominantly private character and opened its gates to the residents of Rome every day of the week except Monday. This implemented the original desire of the founder, Scipione, as is revealed in a memorial tablet in the wall behind the *palazzo*, "*Va dove vuoi, chiedi ciò che vuoi, esci quando vuoi: più che per il proprietario, qui tutto è allestito per l'ospite. . .*" (Go where you will, ask what you will, leave when you will. Here, everything is made ready not for the owner but for the guest). For Villa Borghese, it was the beginning of a magnificent, intense, season.

It was where Romans went for cheerful picnics, singing, games, and dancing during the *ottobrate romane* festivities. These were the days of the

Confraternita Nazarena, and the Deutsche Romer, groups of artists from northern Europe seeking to capture the light of Rome and the Agro Romano countryside. A successful *osteria*, or bar, was opened at the Casino dell'Orologio by one Stefano Giovannini. Piazzale di Siena was the scene of the Cuccagna fairs, military bands, bingo, and lotteries like the charity draw for children orphaned in the cholera epidemic of 1842. Marcantonio V Borghese instituted open-air fairs to educate the populace to return to the soil, as part of a carefully thought-out political and economic program. In 1849, during the interlude of the Roman Republic, the gardens, its buildings, and its follies were severely damaged by the bombardments of the French. After the restoration of the papacy's temporal power, there was a brief period of recovery but this was destined to be short-lived.

The storming of Porta Pia in 1870 ushered in a new era. Rome became the capital of the Kingdom of Italy. The Borgheses, who had close links with the papal court, closed the villa's gates, to

Facing:
In the eighth hall of the Galleria Borghese, visitors can admire a youthful work by Caravaggio, the *Boy with a Basket of Fruit*. The painting was finished in 1594.

Left:
Detail of a wall decorated in the neoclassical taste and graced by a herm, a valuable archaeological piece belonging to the Borghese collection.

Below:
Titian painted his celebrated *Venus Blindfolding Cupid* in 1565. The painting hangs in the same hall as another masterpiece by the same artist, *Sacred and Profane Love*.

open them only for a few hours at a time, in the presence of guards. On 12 May 1885, Marcantonio Borghese ordered the gardens to be closed. The local authority protested and the court ruled in favor of the citizenry. There was to be free access to Villa Borghese on Tuesdays, Thursdays, and Saturdays. Entrance to the *Giardin del Lago* would cost twenty-five *centesimi*. Weighed down by financial difficulties, the family was forced to sell the complex, just as previously they had sold off bas reliefs, statues, and even Asprucci's old double flight of steps and the balustrade of the *piazzale*. The government decided in 1900 to purchase the villa in commemoration of King Umberto I, assassinated at Monza by the anarchist, Gaetano Bresci. The property was subsequently donated to the city of Rome to become a public park, on condition that it should be renamed Villa Umberto I. However, the people of Rome continued to call it Villa Borghese. The entire Borghese art collection also passed to the Italian authorities, to be kept in the *casino*. Villa Borghese was no longer a private residence, although some of the buildings in the grounds remained in private hands. The Fortezzuola belonged to the sculptor Pietro Canonica, later becoming a museum dedicated to the artist, and Palazzina Lubin was also privately owned.

Now accessible to one and all, the estate has undergone a predictable decline as a result of pollution, thefts, and repeated acts of vandalism. Recent

restoration ended a few years ago, having dragged on for fourteen years. The original *marmorino romano* finish has been restored to the facades and the reconstruction of the great seventeenth-century double-flight staircase at the front has given the ancient residence a new lease of life. The gallery has been radically renewed to highlight the splendor of its decoration and the unique treasure trove of art it houses. Set at the heart of a vast museum complex, Villa Borghese is graced by fountains, monuments, sculptures, and has more exhibition space in the grounds at the Museo Canonica, the Casina delle Rose, used for contemporary exhibitions, and the Casina di Raffaello, earmarked as part of the Museo di Villa Borghese. Moreover, the property stretches toward the neighboring Museo Etrusco at Villa Giulia and the Galleria Nazionale d'Arte Moderna.

PALAZZO COLONNA
ROME, LAZIO

"In the oppressive Rome of the baroque age, this externally disappointing *palazzo* and its regal interior was a brilliant beacon, a busy place run by a proud, irritable master who was also a generous, discriminating patron, and head of the family held to be the most ancient and 'important' in the city. Colonna was a personality whose name was synonymous with magnificence." This is how Eduard A. Safarik began his essay on Palazzo Colonna for the catalogue of a remarkable exhibition entitled *Fasto Romano* (Roman Ostentation), held in the sixteenth-century halls of Palazzo Sacchetti in Via Giulia in May and June, 1991. That Roman ostentation, "the now austere, now joyfully refined, yet invariably regal elegance, characteristic of a culture that had shown its mettle at Rome in the greater and lesser arts during the seventeenth and eighteenth centuries," was hailed by the great Giuliano Briganti in the same catalogue as at last reasserting its standing. However, our journey begins long before the baroque age, in the fateful year A.D. 1000. Palazzo Colonna was one of the landmarks of Rome, right from its obscure medieval beginnings, when what was then the tower of the counts of Tuscolo was the scene of bloody power struggles among the barons, and even of insistent threats to papal authority. Sciarra Colonna was one of the protagonists of the "Outrage at Anagni." This incident signaled the decline of Boniface VIII, the pope who had installed his family, the Caetanis, in the Colonna's area of influence, at Torre delle Milizie. By the thirteenth century, the Colonnas had turned the tables, regaining supremacy over the commune of Rome and holding the city in their sway during the so-called "Babylonian captivity" of the popes at Avignon. After the solemn coronation with a laurel wreath of Petrarch, on the Capitol at Easter 1341, the elderly Stefano Colonna, Roman senator and vicar of Robert of Anjou, was to host the

extravagant private reception to celebrate the Tuscan poet's triumph.

The tower was rebuilt in 1424 during the papacy of the Colonna pope, Martin V, when the complex was extended to incorporate several other buildings into a papal residence. Situated adjacent to a church dedicated to the Holy Apostles Philip and James, Palazzo Colonna acquired enormous prestige as the residence of a reigning pope. In the late fifteenth century, Cardinal Pietro

Riario, nephew of another celebrated Renaissance pope, Savona-born Sextus IV, restructured a house on the other side of the church that had belonged to the learned Greek cardinal, Bessarion. The new building was symmetrically offset by another small *palazzo*, erected in a *viridarium*, or garden, at the foot of the Quirinal hill by another "nephew cardinal," Giuliano della Rovere, in the space behind Palazzo Colonna in line with the apse of the church of Santi Apostoli. The Colonnas were thus surrounded by other families' properties that prevented them from extending their own *palazzo*. Nevertheless, all good things come to those who wait. In 1506, the marriage of Lucrezia della Rovere, niece of the cardinal Giuliano della Rovere who was elected to the papacy as Julius II, to Marcantonio Colonna brought with it the neighboring property as a wedding gift from the pope himself. Its

structures were provisionally connected to the fifteenth-century residence of Martin V.

The remains of the grotesque decoration by Pinturicchio on the vaults of Giulio della Rovere's *palazzina* can still be seen in one of the splendidly furnished rooms that were occupied until recently by Princess Isabelle Colonna. For the Colonnas, the Renaissance was the age of the great warriors, the *condottieri*, such as Prospero (1452–1523) and his cousin Fabrizio (1450–1520). Other branches of the family tree reveal Ascanio (1495–1555) and grandson Marcantonio II (1535–1584), the hero of Lepanto, the naval battle that inflicted a severe blow to Ottoman expansion in Europe. *Colonna, Impero, Libertà* (Colonna, Empire, Liberty), the motto of a provocative feast given the previous year by Cardinal Pompeo Colonna, was the war cry of the family's mercenaries as they attacked the Vatican in 1526 to depose the Medici pope, Clement VII, guilty of being hostile to the imperial faction to which the Colonnas belonged. It was Pompeo, nominated vice chancellor of the Church for his decisive role in the election of the Medici pope, who in 1523, obtained a regal tribute from the newly crowned Clement, receiving him in the family residence during his procession to the Lateran.

Resident at the *palazzo* at the time was the Marquess of Mantua, Isabella d'Este, who had sought refuge there with many other aristocrats, gentlewomen, prelates, and ambassadors during the horrors of the Sack of Rome by the Constable de Bourbon and his Lutheran (*Landsknechts*) in May 1527. The military and political glory of the Colonnas under the imperial eagle of the Hapsburgs was bound up with the history of the Kingdom of Naples, to which the family gave six viceroys, obtaining in 1515 the prestigious title of great constable. Nor should we forget the poet Vittoria Colonna, wife of Charles V's general, Ferdinando d'Avalos. The mystically inclined Vittoria, the driving force behind a cultural group suspected of heresy, as well as the friend and platonic lover of Michelangelo, ended her days in the convent in Via della Mercede. Balls, theatrical spectacles, and banquets followed each other against a backdrop of fast-shifting alliances, poisonings, abrupt changes of strategy, and memorable military exploits as the halls of Palazzo Colonna reflected the unfolding

contradictions of the sixteenth century.
Nevertheless, the various buildings in the
complex remained detached from each
other, and even the *viridarium,* or
pleasure garden, had an air of neglect,
despite having been described during the
Age of Humanism as *pulcherrimum,* or
very beautiful.

Between 1611 and 1618, Filippo I
Colonna at last began to lay out the area
as a garden, creating various terraced
levels marked off by imposing box
hedges and flowerbeds. The levels were
linked by graceful flights of steps and
fountains. Palazzo Colonna's golden age,
however, began with the arrival of
Lorenzo Onofrio Colonna. In 1654, he
commissioned Antonio del Grande to
bring the various buildings together in a
single edifice. He gave the facade in the
courtyard a series of arches, now bricked
up, leading them to a central unit and
linking the *palazzo* to the garden with
bridges over what today is Via della
Pilotta. At this point, among picaresque
baroque notes and melancholy hints
reminiscent of Lully, there arrived on the
scene the most fascinating and
tumultuous figures in the centuries-long
history of Palazzo Colonna.

Maria Mancini, niece of the
powerful cardinal Mazarin and married by
proxy to the constable, Lorenzo Onofrio,
loved excess, high society, passion, and
adventure, as did her equally restless
sisters. Maria's career took her from a
relatively humble household in Rome to
the magnificence of the Louvre, where
she won the heart of the young Louis
XIV, and to Pisa, where she died in 1715.
She lived a life as exciting as any novel of
intrigue and adventure. Last of the
pretentious savants known as the
Precieuses de l'Hotel de Rambouillet, Maria
was a romantic, a libertine, and a
generous, if incautious, socializer. She
crossed and recrossed Europe like
refugee, in pomp, poverty, and a
spectacular firework display of scandals,
dramatic turns of events, and religious
conversions, clinging tightly to the
enormous, and enormously celebrated,
pearls given to her by the Sun King when
they were lovers. Rome was simply too
small for her ambition. Raised as an
uninhibited *Fille de France*, and
accustomed to the ceremony and

225

Facing:
Visitors can admire a number of major works on one of the walls in the *Sala Grande*, including *Saint Paul the Hermit* by Guercino, an *Assumption of the Virgin* from the workshop of Rubens, and *Christ in Limbo* by a follower of Alessandro Allori.

Below right:
This wall in the *Sala della Colonna Bellica* offers: in the top left-hand corner, a *Portrait of Lucrezia Tomacelli Colonna* attributed to van Dyck; and, on the right, from the top down, *Night* by Ghirlandaio, the *Temptations of Saint Anthony* from the school of Hieronymus Bosch, and Bronzino's *Venus, Cupid, and Satyr*. The baroque gilt console tables, supported by Moors, also allude to the victory over the Ottomans at Lepanto.

putti by Carlo Maratta and Mario de' Fiori, and through the gallery's endless series of artistic masterpieces from the sixteenth to the late seventeenth centuries. The route is adorned with Venetian chandeliers, elaborately decorated cabinets that are in fact miniature pieces of architecture, consoles supported by Moorish prisoners, gilt stuccoes, busts, and classical sculptures scattered throughout the various rooms.

The collection of paintings is quite extraordinary. Assembled over the generations and centuries, it was constantly expanded, except for the enforced sale of a few major works during the Napoleonic period. In 1730, Fabrizio Colonna commissioned Nicolò Michetti to erect the facade facing onto Santi Apostoli and thirty years later, Cardinal Girolamo Colonna entrusted Paolo Posi with the task of decorating the part of the building overlooking Via della Pilotta. The *palazzo* took on the appearance we know today, delimited by the piazza, the side of the church, Via della Pilotta, and what is now Via XXIV Maggio, arranged round the courtyard

sophisticated etiquette of the French court, Maria had little time for the petty prejudice and hypocritical conventions of the Eternal City.

The birth of her first child, Filippo II Colonna, on April 7, 1663, became the pretext for an extravagant bedstead, designed by one of Gian Lorenzo Bernini's most gifted pupils, the Austrian Johann Paul Schor. The original is no longer extant but a contemporary print survives to show us what it must have looked like. Her triumphal *lit de parade*, well worthy of the fame of its illustrious occupant, as the Swedish architect and gentleman, Nikodemus Tessin, related toward the end of the seventeenth century, "comprised a shell drawn by sea horses and driven by mermaids while cupids held the back with strings of pearls, carved in the round, painted in imitation bronze and gilt. Over the entire composition was a gold and purple brocade with gold fringes. Two statues of Fame and other young people seem to be attaching the cloth to the roof in an apparently haphazard and asymmetrical fashion. The horses prancing through the waves and the mermaids, alluding to the Colonna family, represented the birth of Venus." The allegory hints at the family's naval victories, of which Marcantonio Colonna's triumph at Lepanto was emblematic. It is echoed in the famous gallery completed by Girolamo Fontana and solemnly inaugurated by Filippo II Colonna in 1703. The vaults are decorated sumptuously with frescoes, completed between 1675 to 1678 by Filippo Gherardi and Giovanni Coli, that celebrate the exploits of the Colonna family, especially Marcantonio, the victor over the Turks. The gallery is transformed into a glorification of the house, from the *Sala della Colonna Bellica*, to the *Sala di Martino V*. The celebration continues on the decorative floors of colored marble, baroque mirrors painted with flowers and

Left:
A view of the *Sala dell'Apoteosi di Martino V.*

Below:
The Bean Eater (1583–84) by Annibale Caracci is conserved in the *Sala dell'Apoteosi di Martino V.* Together with the *Butcher's Shop* (1582–83) and the *Crucifixion* (1583), it is considered to be one of the artist's most important masterpieces.

court after the revolutionary Second Vatican Council. When the temporal power of the papacy collapsed in 1870, the Colonnas did not retire from public life in the city. Prospero and Fabrizio Colonna became senators of the young Kingdom of Italy. Prospero was also mayor of Rome on two occasions between 1899 and 1919, presiding over a moderate administration. Piero was governor of Rome from 1936 to 1939. Until not very many years ago, the fascinating Princess Isabelle Sursock Colonna dominated the social scene in Rome, as she had done for more than half a century.

According to a popular superstition, there was a curse on Palazzo Colonna until 1855, which caused it to shiver on its foundations on June 28 of each year, the eve of the feast of Saint Peter and Saint Paul. The reason was the anathema pronounced by the pope on the king of Naples for having annulled, in 1777, the customary annual tribute of a *chinea*, a white horse brought by the king's constable, prince Colonna, who also brought a gift of 7,000 ducats. The excommunication was lifted in 1855 by Pius IX but the Colonnas appear to have given it little thought, pursuing their magnificent career, indifferent to the chaotic passage of time and events.

with a great symbolic column standing in the middle of its trees and parterres. Two low buildings face onto the piazza, dominated on the corner of Via IV Novembre by what used to be the Coffee House, and is now a wax museum. On the third floor is a room with an eight-sided vault decorated with Francesco Mancini's *Tale of Cupid and Psyche*.

As a recent, historic reception to celebrate the family's thousand-year history demonstrated, the Colonnas have been extraordinarily successful in maintaining the splendor of their residence and the fame of their aristocratic house. In 1816, they were the first of Rome's noble families to renounce feudal rights over their vast estates. Leading members of the Roman aristocracy, the Colonnas were from the seventeenth century "assistants to the papal throne," a hereditary office abolished in 1970 by Paul VI, during his modernization of the Vatican

ROYAL PALACE (REGGIA)
CASERTA, CAMPANIA

Commissioned in 1751 by King Charles III of Bourbon from the architect Luigi Vanvitelli, son of the celebrated Dutch landscape painter, Gaspar Van Wittel, the Reggia or Royal Palace of Caserta, as Francesco Fariello observed in his in *L'Architettura dei Giardini* (The Architecture of Gardens), "marks the most felicitous conclusion of the Italian and French experiences, combined by a single creative genius in a clear vision of the potential offered by the site. The open landscape faces south toward the plain and the coast. It is closed to the north by a semicircle of hills covered by dense vegetation."

The immense, scenic park and equally vast, solemn palace at Caserta are indivisibly linked as symbols of the prestige of Charles of Bourbon's new monarchy. The son of Philip V of Spain, who was himself the grandson of Louis XIV of France, Charles was a further piece in the strategic jigsaw puzzle put together by the Navarre-Bourbon dynasty in the seventeenth and eighteenth centuries. Henry IV had ascended to the throne of France, the house had established itself firmly on the international scene thanks to the achievements of the Sun King, and it was now advancing steadily toward one of Europe's leading Catholic thrones. Charles completely reorganized his kingdom, curbing the clergy's excessive power and undermining the feudal system. He promoted an economic, artistic, and moral renaissance, fostering the elaboration of a valid town plan for Naples and an enormous expansion in the civil building stock. Caserta, the Versailles of the kings of Naples, was built for official ceremonies, but was also intended as a better protected home for the royal family and court, after Naples was threatened with bombardment by the British fleet in 1742, to force Charles to remain neutral in the War of the Austrian Succession.

Nine years later, in 1751, the great estate of Caserta was acquired for that purpose from the Princess Gaetani di Sermoneta. The architect chosen was Luigi Vanvitelli, who at the time was working on the restoration of the sanctuary at Loreto. After Benedict XIV granted dispensation in 1750, Vanvitelli was hired to work at Caserta. His plans were presented for approval on November 22 and January 20 1752, the monarch's birthday. The king himself laid the first stone, on top of which Vanvitelli placed another with the apotropaic inscription *"Stet domus et solium et soboles borbonia donec/ad superos propria vi lapis redeat"* (May this house and threshold and the scions of the Bourbons stand, until this stone shall return to the heavens by its own force).

The epic building work slowed down in 1759, when Charles left to be crowned king of Spain, and they were brought to a complete standstill in 1764 by epidemic and famine. Work recommenced the following year. Vanvitelli's career as the favorite architect of the Bourbons of Naples was not always straightforward. We need only recall his deft reply to Queen Maria Amalia, when in 1756, perhaps mindful of the exotic fantasies of northern Europe and especially the taste for chinoiserie in her birthplace, Dresden, the capital of the Saxon states, she asked him for "something completely Chinese." Vanvitelli, a classicist who was anything but attracted to the whimsical Rocaille chinoiseries so popular in the Europe of the day, answered ironically, but with all the flattery and respectful poise of a perfect courtier, "I shall transform myself into a Chinese Architect, as if I were building for the Emperor of China." In

1773, Luigi Vanvitelli passed away. The following year, the fabric of the building was completed under the direction of Luigi's son, Carlo, who also supervised decoration of the interior. Carlo had to deal with financial difficulties and court politics and was unable to implement his father's design. The original plans called for a central dome, with turrets at the corners, and accommodation for the guards facing the elliptical perimeter of the *piazza* in front of the palace.

Ferdinando IV loved Caserta, spending each spring and autumn there in a magnificent succession of ceremonial events, hunts, feasts, banquets, and receptions. The *Re Bomba*, or Bomb King, as he was known to the populace, died at Caserta in 1859, the year before the Bourbon states were finally dissolved and annexed to the Kingdom of Italy after a plebiscite, which took place under Francesco II, the unfortunate

Facing:
The great staircase is made up of a central flight that splits into two parallel flights, both leading to the vestibule.

Franceschiello. Caserta belonged to the crown of Italy until 1919, when it passed to state ownership. The palace suffered bomb damage and then, in 1943, the Reggia became the Allied Mediterranean Headquarters. On April 27 1945, the instrument of local surrender for German troops in Italy was signed here. The construction is in brick and travertine stone from Santo Iorio, and decorated with marble from Carrara and the south of Italy. Built to a rectangular plan, 810 by 623 feet, it is arranged in four courtyards, also rectangular, and is 135 feet high. There are five floors, including a basement level for kitchens, pantries, and cellars. The 1,200 rooms are served by thirty-four staircases and there are 1,742 windows. The front rises from an ashlar base bearing a colossal order of *lesenes* and fluted engaged columns. It culminates in an attic, itself crowned by a balustrade that is broken up by a brief central tympanum panel. The three entrances were intended to be watched over by allegorical statues, which were never completed. Inside, the spacious three-aisle central gallery opens out—the central aisle is for carriages and the outer two for pedestrians—penetrating right through the edifice and focusing the observer's eye. This carefully constructed perspective. It continues an imaginary line along the main avenue from Naples, now intersected by the railway tracks. In line with the main entrance, it carried on through the park to end at the *mise en scène* of the *Grande Cascata*, or Great Cascade. The niches of the octagonal lower vestibule, halfway along the gallery, house a colossal copy of the Farnese Hercules, as well as statues of Venus and Germanicus by Andrea Violani, and those of Apollo and Antinous from ancient models, carved by Pietro Solari. After climbing the ceremonial double staircase in Trapani lumachella stone, with its white marble lions by Pietro Solari and Paolo Persico, and niche-mounted allegorical statues, the visitor reaches the octagonal upper vestibule. Its vaulted ceiling rests on eight trapezoid pillars, flanked by twenty-four Ionic columns in Gargano breccia stone.

The Palatine Chapel, inaugurated in 1784, again draws inspiration from Versailles. Its colonnade stands on a high stylobate, highlighting its role both as a court church dedicated to Christian worship and a setting for the complicated

rituals of Bourbon protocol. The Royal Apartments reveal a mixed eighteenth and nineteenth-century ambience.

The rooms by Carlo Vanvitelli, completed between 1779 and 1790 in a supremely refined contemporary style, blend the last flourishes of rocaille grace with the first hints of neoclassicism. The movement's international fortunes were founded at Naples, thanks to the early scientifically organized excavation campaigns at Herculaneum around the fourth decade of the eighteenth century. These followed the first accidental finds made at the initiative of the Austrian regent, prince d'Elboeuf, from 1711 to 1712 and 1716.

Ferdinando's style, which is roughly similar to the French Louis Seize idiom, evolved in a sophisticated milieu of cabinetmakers, ornamental painters, engravers, and ceramists eager to transpose into a rich eighteenth-century decorative vocabulary the archeological remains, allegories, and imagery of the classical world that was emerging from the oblivion of the past. The *Appartamento Vecchio*, or Old Apartment, lies to the left of the *Sala di Alessandro* (Alexander Room). Behind the latter is the Terrae Motus exhibition of contemporary art put together by the inspired Neapolitan gallerist, Lucio Amelio, while the *Appartamento Vecchio* itself is a triumph of white and gold in its décor and in the superb carvings, most by Gennaro Di Fiore. The wall hangings demonstrate the excellent quality of the silk fabrics from neighboring factory at

San Leucio, also founded by the Bourbons. In the *Sala Ellittica* (Elliptical Room), the scenic *Presepe Reale*, or Royal Nativity Scene, tells of the exquisitely Neapolitan passion for this special form of art. The genre reached its apogee in the eighteenth century, involving rich bourgeois and aristocratic patrons, high-ranking prelates, and even the monarchs, Charles III and Maria Amalia.

The royal family took a personal interest in the layout of these varied, theatrical compositions, more secular than sacred in nature, and in the creation of costumes and accessories for the figures. The shepherds and animals of the *Presepe*

Facing above:
One of the palace's small living rooms. Building costs ran to six million ducats and a large number of slaves and Muslim prisoners, captured in the Mediterranean and Libya, were employed during construction.

Facing below:
The *Sala di Marte* was reserved for "Title-holders, Barons of the Kingdom, Officers, Soldiers, and Foreign Envoys." It was created by Joachim Murat during the Napoleonic kingdom.

Left:
The vestibule is built to an octagonal plan. The richly decorated vault is divided into rigorous geometrical spaces.

Below:
The first gallery facing the great staircase. The niche contains a statue by Tommaso Solari of Charles of Bourbon astride a lion.

Reale were completed in the eighteenth and nineteenth centuries by Naples' most celebrated sculptors, such as Giovanni Battista Polidoro, Nicola Somma, the Vassallos, Francesco Gallo, Salvatore Franco, Lorenzo Mosca, Giuseppe Gori, and Francesco and Camillo Celebrano. The fervid creativity of late eighteenth-century Naples is apparent in the *Appartamento Vecchio* with its huge Venetian mirrors, allegorical frescoes by Fedele Fischetti, and the celebrated tempera paintings by Jacob Philip Hackert of royal locations, the kingdom's ports, hunts and military maneuvers at the time of Ferdinando IV.

Equally impressive is the extraordinary furniture, made by Nicola and Pietro Di Fiore from 1796 to 1798, the classical imitation vases by the Giustiniani ceramic factory in Naples, the Murano chandeliers and the superb one by Gennaro Di Fiore and Antonio Serio for the *Gabinetto degli Specchi* (Mirror Room). The nineteenth-century interiors, especially in the *Appartamento Nuovo* (New Apartment) and the *Appartamento del Re* (King's Apartment), are

Left:
The throne room was completed only in 1845 by Gaetano Genovese. The geometric patterns and octagon-framed rose decorations of the floor provide a delightful counterpoint to the ceiling frescoes by Gennaro Maldarelli.

Below:
A significant decorative feature is this gilt statue of History by Tita Angelini and Tommaso Arnaud. It stands over the throne, itself decorated with winged lions, flowers, and cornucopias.

characterized by an overall Empire note. The ambience in these rooms has a grandiose classical idiom. The paintings, commissioned from academic artists like Giuseppe Cammarano, focus on mythological, historical, and celebratory themes whereas the furniture is inspired by French models and the production of Jacob as well as by the style of Percier and Fontaine.

The Bourbon restoration is evident in various pieces in the neo-baroque, revival-oriented, idiom of the enormous throne room, designed by Gaetano Genovese from 1844 to 45. The frieze relates the history of Naples in forty-four medallions, each portraying a king. Unsurprisingly, the Napoleonic "usurpers," Joseph Bonaparte and Joachim Murat, are not included. The Prince of Salina, the hero of Giuseppe Tomasi di Lampedusa's

celebrated novel, *Il Gattopardo (The Leopard),* tells of his occasional visits as a Sicilian nobleman to the "slovenly" court at Naples, comparing the kingdom to the Reggia at Caserta. His definition may be unfair and excessively caustic, but it is highly effective, "magnificent architecture, disgusting furniture."

At Caserta, there was also a horseshoe-plan court theater with five tiers of seating. It was completed by Luigi Vanvitelli in 1769, with pink stone cladding, alabaster columns, and a vault decorated by the painter Crescenzo Gamba with a representation of *Apollo Crushing the Python.* The immense park, sweetest of the delights offered by the Bourbon royal estates, spreads out to embrace the surrounding countryside. The first designs for the gardens hinted at Le Notre at Vaux-le-Vicomte and featured broad terraces linked by stairs, retracing the absolute, Leibniz-inspired art of the

Facing:
The bathroom of Francesco II dates from 1825. The granite bathtub is adorned with two stone lion's heads.

Facing far right:
This bathroom is thought to have belonged to Queen, Maria Carolina, consort of Ferdinando I. It is elegantly decorated in the neoclassical idiom with gilt stucco and frescoes, inspired by archeological discoveries.

Left:
The *lit en bateau* bed, writing desk, chest of drawers, and Empire chairs in Murat's bedroom were from the Portici palace.

Below:
The *Camera di Francesco II,* dominated by a mahogany and gilt bronze bed, takes its name from Ferdinando II's successor, enthroned in 1859 and deposed in 1860. The room's sophisticated decoration dates from the years of Murat's rule.

at Naples in the new international cultural milieu of the late eighteenth century. The atmosphere in the city was modern and open. The decades after the mid-eighteenth century witnessed the arrival of Voltaire, the Abbé de Saint Non, Pompeo Batoni, Mengs, Hubert Robert, Tischbein, Angelika Kauffmann, Hackert, Thomas Jones, and, of course, Goethe. Marie Caroline gathered around her a brilliant and highly influential circle. Attracted by the Enlightenment and by Freemasonry, the queen was a close friend of the very beautiful Emma Lyon, the sensuous adventuress who had yet to embark on her affair with Admiral Nelson. At the time, she was the young wife of the cultured British resident, Sir William Hamilton, an enthusiastic vulcanologist, collector of antiquities, and subscriber to Giovan Battista Piranesi's prints. The uninhibited Emma, who would become, with the queen and the

éminence grise Cardinal Ruffo, the driving spirit behind the bloody suppression of the revolt, was universally known for her celebrated, archeologically-inspired *tableaux vivants*, which were enjoyed by Goethe, among others, during his stay in the Bourbon capital in 1787.

Marie Caroline was keen to emulate her sister, the queen of France, Marie Antoinette, who had commissioned from Hubert Robert the picturesque village of Hameau at Versailles. She also wished to surprise her bored husband with delicate early fruits from her own garden. Graefer began work in the hills in the northeast of the royal park, which was especially fertile thanks to the water supplied by the *acquedotto carolino*, and thus suitable for the cultivation of tropical plants. By 1792, progress was good and a vast plantation of rare conifers had been established, as well as a huge variety of exotic plants that were little known and

Grand Siècle at the French royal parks at Versailles and Marly. Later, Luigi Vanvitelli pivoted the composition on the five successive waterfalls, framed by a double row of vegetation in the monumentally extended central area. Although the garden is simplified with respect to the original conception, it still shows its solemn Enlightenment-inspired dedication to the fortunate kingdom of Charles III. The monarch's strong personality is echoed in the statues around the fountains, whose hunting motif symbolizes the great Bourbon king's passion for the pursuit. An abundance of water, supplied by the *acquedotto carolino* water supply system specially designed by Vanvitelli, brings to life grotesques, groups of statues, and scenic stairs to culminate in the theatrical élan of the vast basin that receives the great cascade. It is here that the dramatic, dynamic groups of Diana and Acteon, by Angelo Brunelli, Paolo Persico, Solari, and others face each other to provide a visual and scenic fulcrum for the entire park. Vanvitelli, as Cesare de Seta observed, "ignores the great discoveries at Pompeii and Herculaneum . . . and shows in his every act that he is insensitive to the antiquarian culture that is the essential leaven of the neoclassical age." But in 1786, thirteen years after Vanvitelli's death, there was a dramatic change of scene. Queen Marie Caroline asked the director of London's Kew Gardens for the services of the British nurseryman and botanist, John Andrew Graefer, from whom she commissioned a new garden for Caserta. Graefer took up his position

Above:
The lovely English garden is further beautified by tropical plants and statues like this one of Venus about to bathe in the pool.

Facing:
To ensure that the garden's fountains and pools would have plenty of water, Vanvitelli spent more than sixteen years making excavations and constructing the *acquedotto carolino* water supply system.

Right and below:
Charles II wished to create a palace and garden that would vie in splendor with the one at Versailles. The photographs show details of two of the many fountains with which Vanvitelli made the king's dream come true.

almost impossible to find in Europe. Until 1798, examples arrived from all over the world to be planted, and included the *Camellia japonica* that Graefer obtained through his acquaintance with the Swedish doctor and botanist, Thunberg, who worked for the Dutch East India Company. The English garden lies on gently sloping ground and is closed off by the arboretum. Shaded areas and watercourses combine to conjure up images of genuine landscape art, poised between neoclassicism and the burgeoning romantic idiom. The *Bathing Venus*, the exedra-style portico, and the carefully orchestrated arrangement of false remains festooned in myrtle and ivy mark out a "picturesque journey" that evoke Piranesi's engravings of the Roman remains yielded by the earth at Herculaneum, Stabia, and Pompeii.

PALAZZO REALE DI CAPODIMONTE
NAPLES, CAMPANIA

Facing:
One of the rooms in the museum during the exhibition dedicated to the Bourbons.

Below:
The *palazzo* was built for Charles III. Work started in 1738. This photograph shows the inner colonnade.

Both the Kingdom of Naples and the Papal States considered the artistic heritage to be an integral part of their civil identity. "In the south of Italy," Salvatore Settis, director of the Scuola Normale at Pisa, wrote, "it was the 'reactionary' Bourbons who laid the regulatory foundations for the safeguarding works of art, followed by the even more 'reactionary' Papal States." A proclamation by Charles III Bourbon in 1755 confirmed that "the Provinces, of which this Kingdom of Naples is composed, have at all times administered in great abundance rare monuments of antiquity, statues, paintings, medals, and vases." The text pointed out that no care had been taken to collect or preserve such monuments, and that "all the most precious objects unearthed have been removed from the Kingdom."

The decree communicated to the king's subjects his strict order banning the exportation and sale of antiquities, prescribing custodial sentences for both commoners and nobles who transgressed. The ban, which also covered "ancient pictures" and "worked stones and marble," was renewed in 1766 and 1769 by Ferdinando IV, who had succeeded Charles to the Spanish throne in 1759. A far less brilliant and enlightened ruler than his father, Ferdinando did show a special, even jealous, sensitivity for the artistic and archeological treasures his kingdom contained in such abundance. In 1822, further decrees were published banning the demolition of buildings "of noble architecture," which entailed the nomination of a *Commissione di Antichità e Belle Arti* (Commission for Antiquities and Fine Art).

Ferdinando, husband of the authoritarian Marie Caroline of Hapsburg-Lorraine, was the idol of the colorful populace of Naples' lower orders and much preferred hunting to exercising regal power. In 1787, he ignored the severe laws of the Papal States, and the equally unequivocal dispositions in the

1587 will of his ancestor, Alessandro Farnese, transferring to Naples all the sculptures in the Farnese collections from the dowry of his paternal grandmother, Elisabetta Farnese. The works were stripped from the various residences of the august dukes of Parma, including Palazzo Farnese in Rome. Notwithstanding this last, not entirely orthodox, episode, we have said enough to make at least a contribution to restoring the good name of the Neapolitan Bourbons, a dynasty often accused of poor administration, weakness, irresponsibility, a complete lack of any global political vision, and disinterest for the miserable condition of much of southern Italy's population. In the mid-nineteenth century, Alexandre Dumas, who had many reasons of his own not to like the dynasty, made devastating accusations about the monarchs of Naples as the shaky structure of the Kingdom of Naples was about to crumble to nothing. Yet the Bourbons, especially the enlightened Charles III, left an ineffaceable, and very vivid, mark that is indelibly engraved on Naples' innermost soul.

The extravagant, excessive, and exquisitely baroque story of the Bourbons is a contradictory mishmash of splendor, squalor, enlightened rule, neglect, and attacks of absolutism. Denials, betrayals, and concessions of reform alternated with regal pomp, hotheaded populism, cruelty, fear, suspicion, pride, sentimentalism, and a sense of identity. In 1860, the final curtain fell on what had been, since 1735, the enthronement of Charles III and the end of the Spanish vice regency, the Kingdom of the Two Sicilies. The saga had lasted just over 130 years. It was a period of light and shade that combined the conquests of the Enlightenment with extraordinary artistic and musical activity. Absolute monarchy clashed with libertarian movements that challenged its firmly blinkered refusal to accept that the world was changing. Cynicism and chivalrous illusions accompanied the Ancien Régime to its grave. Charles III had brought to the new throne of Naples an uncommon energy. His cosmopolitan court soon rivaled Venice, Paris, London, and Vienna in the arts, in thought, in music—especially opera—in its fashionable life, and in its social reforms. Charles launched a modern program of reform, encouraging an impressive wave of building that now concentrated on civil edifices instead of religious ones. This was the period when the Reggia and its gardens were built at Caserta. The royal palace at Portici was completed, as were the Albergo dei Poveri, the San Carlo theater, and the royal estates at Cardito and Carditello. The Manifattura Ceramica porcelain works opened at Capodimonte, and silk mills at San Leucio, to satisfy the

increasing internal demand for luxury goods. Excavations began at Herculaneum, Stabia, and Pompeii. Superb villas and country residences began to appear on the sublimely beautiful slopes of Posillipo. Palazzo Reale di Capodimonte stands on the panoramic high ground after which it is named. The vast, rectangular complex dominating the city is laid out around three courts and is clearly visible against its intense green backdrop of holm oaks. Charles of Bourbon decided to build it to house the art collections he had inherited from his mother, Elisabetta, last of the Farnese dukes of Parma.

Since the Renaissance pope, Paul III, and his nephew, Cardinal Alessandro, the Farneses had been generous patrons of the arts, amassing spectacular collections of paintings, sculpture, precious objects, and classical antiquities. The Farnese treasures were originally stored at Palazzo Reale while they waited

for a fitting final destination. Building began in 1738 under the supervision of the architect Giovanni Antonio Medrano, working with Antonio Canevari. Both came from Rome and the partnership was an unhappy one, producing a severe, compact, classically inspired edifice that would be completed only between 1834 and 1838. By 1758 and 1759, when Charles had to leave Naples to be crowned king of Spain, twelve rooms were at last ready to receive *Real Galleria di Parma*. Two of the leading figures in the Naples of King Charles now come into the building's history: the innovative, experimental architect Ferdinando Sanfelice, who was commissioned in 1742 and 1743 to lay out the gardens; and the other great builder of the day, Ferdinando Fuga, engaged in 1765 to continue the work. Joachim Murat, King of Naples during the decade of Napoleonic rule, made Capodimonte his principal residence, transferring the art collections to Palazzo Francavilla at Chiaia. After the restoration, and while work was still in progress, the complex was used as guest accommodation, or for brief visits by the court.

In 1828, the Palazzina dei Principi was completed, in 1833 the third courtyard was added, two years after the two stairs. The years 1836 and 1837 saw the completion of the interior decor and the English garden, designed by Friederich Dehenhardt on the nearest wooded area to the *palazzo*. By 1838, the complex was finished and it was decided to create a picture gallery organized on

more modern lines. After 1860, when the Savoys had arrived, the Royal Armory and collections of porcelain, including the celebrated *Salottino di Portici*, and tapestries were brought here. Ceded to the nation by the crown in 1920, Capodimonte was the residence of the dukes of Aosta, an important cadet branch of the house of Savoy, until 1946, when Italy voted to become a republic. In 1957, the *palazzo* became the home of the Galleries Commission for Campania, and part of the National Museum and

Galleries. Its collection was based on the original nucleus of masterpieces by Venetian, Lombard, and Emilian painters, as well as works by Tuscan and Flemish artists from the Farnese collections.

Donations and acquisitions from the eighteenth or nineteenth centuries or later were incorporated, as was the deposit from Naples' churches, the Department of Prints and Drawings, and an extensive sector dedicated to applied arts. The 1980 earthquake required restoration work, after which the museum was partly opened again to the public in 1995. The third floor was opened in 1999, its new layout designed by Ermanno Guida. From the beginning, the *palazzo* was always a ceremonial royal residence, a purpose it combined with its role as a container for first art collections, then exhibitions. The ancient magnificence of the royal apartments at Capodimonte is attested by the rooms in the Historic Apartments, which are graced for the most part with Empire furniture and pieces from the early nineteenth century. There are rows and rows of portraits of the Bourbons by Francesco Liani, Anton Raphael Mengs, Francisco Goya, Angelika Kauffmann, and Elisabeth Vigée-Lebrun. They are accompanied by likenesses from Napoleonic days by Girodet-Trioson and Gérard, as well as a plaster model for the monument to Letizia Bonaparte, the proud, shrewd, indomitable *Madame Mère*, by Antonio Canova and the neoclassical marble *Night* by Bertel Thorwaldsen. We also find a panel by Jacob for Fontainebleau, floors from Roman villas, tapestries by Gobelins and the Real Manifattura at Naples, and Rocaille furnishings from the days of Charles III made for the various royal residences. There are delightful eighteenth-century sedan chairs and precious clocks, as well as spectacular canvases of eruptions of Vesuvius and night views over the Gulf of Naples by Jean-Jacques Volaire in the sumptuous ballroom, decorated by Salvatore Giusti in the 1830s. There are also academic, historical, *pompier* paintings by Vincenzo Camuccini and eighteenth-century frescoes by Fedele Fischetti from the ceilings of the Palazzo di Sangro at Casacalenda. Nevertheless, porcelain is the star of the show. A collection of more than 3,000 pieces tells the story of Europe's leading porcelain manufacturers during the Enlightenment, from Sèvres to Vienna, Frankenthal, Derby-Chelsea, the Vezzi and Cozzi factories in Venice, Meissen, through to the porcelain factory set up at Capodimonte, thanks to the

matrimonial alliance of Charles III and Maria Amalia of Saxony. Examples illustrate the Rococo virtuosity of Giuseppe Gricci and the classical lines of Filippo Tagliolini. It is graceful, quintessentially Ancien Régime porcelain, pale biscuitware, and services decorated by skilled hands for the tables of the court, such as the stunning *Servizio dell'Oca*, or "Goose Service," from the kilns of Capodimonte. Visitors will note medieval ceramics from Asia Minor and Persia, fifteenth-century Hispano-Moorish

Above:
The portrait of Napoleon I is reproduced on the enameled vase underneath, which dates from about 1810.

Facing:
The ballroom at Capodimonte has a raised minstrel's gallery on four Ionic columns where the musicians would take their places.

majolicas and vases, *albarello* jars, plates, and cups from the leading Italian factories of the sixteenth and seventeenth centuries at Orvieto, Siena, Mantua, Savona, Venice, Bassano and Castelli d'Abruzzo. There are examples of Chinese porcelain from the K'hang Hsi and Chien Lung periods, fiercely contested by eighteenth-century collectors. Then, too, there are Renaissance *bronzetti*, Murano glassware, and Attic and Apulian vases, together making up the universe of the collection donated to the nation in 1958 by the

Neapolitan collector, Mario De Ciccio. This Chamber of Curiosities embraces more than 1,300 items.

Finally, we come to the coup de théâtre, the apogee not only of the sophisticated Naples of Charles III of Bourbon, but also symbolic of the inimitable refinement, the graceful, sparkling *joie de vivre* of Enlightenment Europe, inebriated in the dazzling, dying apotheosis of absolutism. The *Salottino* (or *Gabinetto*) *di Porcellana*, one of the finest examples of chinoiserie in Europe, is a landmark of rocaille that enjoyed outstanding success in the eighteenth century, then in the early decades of the following one. It measures twenty-two by fifteen feet, and nearly seventeen feet high, and its walls are entirely clad in porcelain. More than 3,000 pieces of porcelain from the kilns of the Manifattura di Capodimonte take the place of the *boiseries*, or the lacquered white, gold, or pale colors so dear to the artists of rococo decor. The room is a precious *Marivaudage* of graceful Chinese figures, garlands, and delicate floral designs. From the stucco ceiling hangs a lovely chandelier in porcelain. There are genuine Chinese characters, expressing genuine good wishes to the monarch, on whom the Almighty "bestowed good fortune, blessings, and virtue." Founded by Matteo Ripa, the college took in

students from the Celestial Empire. Chinese advisors were probably involved directly, at least in some stages of its construction. The *Salottino* at Portici is the largest and most significant example anywhere of the use of porcelain for interior decoration. It was completed at the express order of Charles of Bourbon between 1757 and 1759, perhaps under the supervision of Giuseppe Gricci, for the monarch's beloved consort Maria Amalia of Saxony. The princess had arrived in Naples in 1732, bringing as her dowry fully seventeen fabulous services in porcelain made by the Meissen factory that was the envy of contemporary rulers and had been set up by her grandfather, the elector Augustus the Strong. According to some sources, the painted decoration was entrusted to Johannes Sigmund Fischer, and then from 1758, to Luigi Restile, although there is no documentary evidence to confirm this. Set in the king's much-loved royal apartments at Portici, the *Salottino* stayed there until 1866, when it was finally reassembled at Capodimonte because of the stripping and rapid decline of the suburban palace after Naples was annexed to the Kingdom of Italy. Despite the fact that it is one of the eighteenth century's pivotal interiors, as Alvar Gonzalez-Palacios recently observed, the *Gabinetto di Portici* has yet to be studied in depth. It has been

suggested that the overall composition derives from a series of prints by Watteau, but the hypothesis has never been conclusively proved. A similar room was created by Neapolitan workers, again for Charles III, in 1761 at Aranjuez, where the king had set up a new factory, taking with him many of the finest craftsmen from Capodimonte. The name, or rather names, of the designers of the painted decoration and architecture are again shrouded in mystery. Regarding the Aranjuez room, Hugh Honour went so far as to posit the intervention of Giovan Domenico Tiepolo, who at the time was in Spain in the service of Charles III. A few years earlier, Tiepolo had frescoed the so-called Chinese scenes in the *foresteria* building at Villa Valamarana, Vicenza. What we can be sure of is the resounding impression made by the Naples *Gabinetto*, which lasted throughout the eighteenth century.

Emperor Josef II of Austria visited Naples in 1769, his sister Marie Caroline having married King Ferdinando IV. The emperor was lavish in his praise of the *cabinet garni de porcelaine*, and provoked the prompt reaction of his brother-in-law to his inquiry as to whether the *Gabinetto* was a product of the porcelain works of Saxony. The king replied that it was the product "of a factory in this country, which his father had destroyed, taking all the workers with him to Spain."

The *Salottino*, a rare example of rococo whimsy, also enchanted Lalande, a brilliant of the eighteenth century travelers, who remarked about the Bourbon residence at Portici, "I admired there especially the Porcelain Room, which is entirely clad and furnished with the porcelain that used to be made at Capo di Monte. It is one of the most beautiful things I have seen in Italy."

VILLA PALAGONIA
PALERMO, SICILY

Having established Palermo, the second city of the Kingdom of the Two Sicilies, as its headquarters, the Sicilian aristocracy felt a need for town houses and, especially, for residences in which to take refuge from the summer heat. As a result, the semi-abandoned areas outside the city walls, once covered by the luxuriant gardens of the medieval Norman kings, began in the eighteenth century to be occupied by villas set in parks, citrus groves, vineyards, and farmland. One of the most favored areas around Palermo itself was the road that leads up to Monreale, which is still graced by eye-catching baroque constructions, and Piana dei Colli, the valley running from Palermo to Sferracavallo and Mondello, bounded on one side by Monte Pellegrino and on the other by the Gallo and Gibilforni hills. Less numerous, but larger and more imposing, are the residences constructed at this time around the village of Bagheria, eight miles east of Palermo.

Although now abandoned, or increasingly threatened by encroaching illegal urban development, many of the eighteenth-century edifices at Bagheria still stand. Among these are the dramatic architectural complex of Villa Valguarnera, built by Tommaso Maria Napoli between 1709 and 1739, Villa Cattolica, Villa Larderia, and the splendid and still intact Villa Spedalotto.

Until the middle of the seventeenth century, Bagheria was an unprepossessing residential settlement surrounded by farmland. Its history as a resort for the nobility of Palermo began in 1658, when Giuseppe Branciforte, prince of Butera, chose it as his retreat after his retirement from public life. Branciforte, who for many years had been the Spanish viceroy's prime minister, established his new home on a site just above the village itself. A few decades later, in the early eighteenth century, his example was followed by many of the city's noble families. Villa Palagonia was begun in 1715 for Ferdinando Francesco Gravina, prince of Palagonia and marquis of Francofonte, knight of the Toson d'Oro and Grande di Spagna. It was probably built to plans drawn up by the mysterious Dominican Tommaso Maria Napoli. Since the Enlightenment, it has loomed large in the imagination of European visitors, and of those engaged in making the Grand Tour. Work was supervised by architect Agostino Daidone. Related to the prince of Resuttano, and having completed an intense period of study at Rome and Vienna, the Dominican architect intended his design for the residence to be a demonstration of the knowledge he had acquired. For example, he adopted for Villa Palagonia the Mannerist polygonal plan of Palazzo Farnese at Caprarola. Although it did not enjoy the privileged situation of Villa Valguarnera, Villa Palagonia dominated the surrounding landscape from a small hillock and had two entries, formed by the road that ran through it at ground level, as we can in

the eighteenth-century view by Jean Houel, from the Porta dei Giganti and the no longer extant avenue. A lively array of projections emerged from the polygonal plan. Alternate filled volumes and empty spaces made up the two terraces flanking the closed loggia in the middle. On the concave facade opposite, it was the spectacular monumental double staircase that provided a focus of attention. Building work must have been largely complete in 1718, when Procopio Serpotta, son of the gifted sculptor Giacomo, was hired to take care of the stuccowork in the interior.

As early as 1741 to 1745, while work was still under way on the *palazzo* in Palermo's Via Alloro into which the Gravinas had recently moved, the new Prince Ignazio Sebastiano summoned from Trapani Nicolò Troisi to give the villa a chapel and a series of low

two decades, from 1751 to 1772. It was almost certainly L'Avocato who designed the superb multicolored mixed marble floor, dating from 1758, in the covered central loggia. He must also have created the garden and the "avenue of extravagances and bric-a-brac," as it was called by one contemporary, the marquis of Villabianca, prompted by the impressive tufa statues acting out their silent, sibylline story. Mystery, ambiguity, and dreamy deformity are veined with nightmare-like delirium and the fantastical projections of the creator's mind. The long list of illustrious visitors includes the painter and engraver Jean Houel, who arrived in 1777 to propose an interpret-ation of the impressive groups of statues. In his view, they derived from "the stories, fairy tales or novels, or society scenes," of his colleague Louis Ducros, who sketched the monsters grouped

buildings that would be used as stables and storehouses. The building program continued after the prince's death at the insistence of his son and heir, who called in Francesco Ferrigno, the architect of the senate building in Palermo. But the younger Ferdinando Francesco had a very clear vision of what he wanted to build. He found the ideal interpreter and executor for his visionary architectural concepts in Rosario L'Avocato, who is recorded as being in his service for over

together in a tableau along the main avenue and perimeter wall, and of Count Michel-Jean de Borch, author of the *Lettres sur la Sicile e sur l'Ile de Malte* (Letters on Sicily and the Island of Malta). Today, the villa is menaced by the chaotic urban sprawl of Bagheria, although it has still conserved its low adjacent buildings. These, however, were originally the focus of a long entrance avenue alongside which ran walls surmounted by monstrous and grotesque figures.

This detail must have shocked the unfortunate Johann Wolfgang von Goethe when he visited Bagheria on April 9, 1787, following the trail of enlightenment blazed by Winkelmann to the Mediterranean sources of classical beauty. Almost in disgust, he wrote in his journal that the poorly fashioned "figures produced in great numbers" of the "groups on the avenue" had "sprung up with no connection and without any control of the intellect, thrown together

Above:
A medallion with a marble bust of an ancestor graces the *Salone degli Specchi*, covered with trompe l'oeil decoration.

Facing:
The sumptuously adorned *Salone degli Specchi* is marked off by portraits of the principal patrons.

Below:
The elliptical entrance hall is frescoed with feigned architectural features that frame the *Labors of Hercules.*

with no logic or effort at selection. . . ." Around the house, "on ground almost totally covered with grass" like "an abandoned cemetery, lay marble vases decorated with curious patterns . . .dwarfs and monsters . . ." Is this disquieting *mise en scène* the tardy daughter of an eccentric baroque Medusa, or a foretaste of Goya's *Caprichos* and the inventions of early twentieth-century surrealism? It is no coincidence that, like Bomarzo, Villa Palagonia exercised an enormous fascination on Dalí and the Sitwells. Goethe had a vivid memory of the interior, as well as the outside, of the house. He described the sulfurous fantasies and necromantic paraphernalia inside, from the wooden crucifix set horizontally on the chapel vault, a penitent's severed head hanging on a chain from its navel, to the chairs with their irregular legs, the *fauteuils à la de Sade* concealing spikes under their red velvet cushions, and the distorting glass in the windows.

This eighteenth-century collection of accouterments worthy of Bela Lugosi combined dazzle with darkness, and the seedy with the certifiably insane, in an irrational *Wunderkammer* teeming with obscure and inexplicable symbols. Ferdinando Francesco Gravina junior looks as if he would have been a perfect accomplice for the Neapolitan Prince Raimondo di Sangro, his contemporary who was under equally strong suspicion of witchcraft and esotericism. A document from 1753 informs us that sculptors were working at the villa, although no reference is made to the so-called "monsters."

The marble-cutters Agostino Vitagliano, Carmelo Rizzo, Giuseppe Muscarello, and Filippo di Stefano were commissioned to make two fountains, the more complex of which was decorated with *putti*, gryphons, statues, and mascarons that have not survived. The coordinator of the entire architectural and decorative scheme was Rosario L'Avocato, the trusted interpreter of the prince of Palagonia's fertile, albeit diseased, imagination. Gioachino Lanza Tomasi has put forward comparisons with subjects from the contemporary production of Meissen porcelain figures in Saxony, a view endorsed by similarities with eighteenth-century Venetian examples made for gardens and grottoes. What is certain is that the musicians derive from the engravings in a catalogue of musical instruments published in Rome in 1723, the *Gabinetto Armonico, Pieno d'Istromenti Sonori, Indicati, Spiegati e di*

Nuovo Corretti ed Accresciuti dal Padre Filippo Bonanno della Compagnia di Gesù (Harmonic Cabinet Full of Sonorous Instruments, Described, Explained, and Newly Corrected and Enlarged by Father Filippo Bonanno of the Company of Jesus).

Goethe also mentions the celebrated ballroom, or *Salone degli Specchi*, with its vaulted, mirror-covered ceiling. It had very much impressed Patrick Brydone in 1770 but had not been completed seven years later. The polished walls are of imitation colored and jasper marble, their glass-covered paintings achieving surprising trompe-l'oeil effects. There is a liberal sprinkling of medallions with marble busts of the family's forebears. Over all this, the mirrors of the fairy-tale vault are painted with a frothy cornice, which is in turn surmounted by gilt urns and wrinkled at the corners by flamboyant red coral Rocaille shells. A

moralizing maxim reveals the ultimate meaning of the composition of mirrors, alluding to the ineluctable transience of the real world *Specchiati in Quei Cristalli, e nell'Istessa Magnificenza Singolar, Contempla di Fralezza Mortal l'Imago Espressa* (Reflect Thyself in These Glasses and in The Magnificence of Solitude, Contemplate the Image Portrayed of Mortal Frailty). It is a Counter-Reformation intimation of mortality at the height of the century of Voltaire, Rousseau, and d'Alembert. The inventory compiled on the death of Prince Ferdinando Francesco in 1788 bears witness to the villa's lavish furnishings and fittings. In the oval entrance hall, today frescoed with the *Labors of Hercules*, a splendid collection of fifty-four paintings hung among imitation architectural features, which were put there by Salvatore Gravina, Francesco's younger brother and heir, having married his only daughter.

Awaiting their new, neoclassical grotesque decoration, the rooms leading off to the left of the entrance were adorned with paintings of Arcadian and mythological scenes, and landscapes with ancient temples, celebrating the dying moments of rococo in the brocade hangings on the walls. After 1788, Salvatore Gravina appears to have attempted to efface his brother's uncomfortable memory, removing various statues from the garden. He also summoned from Naples the artist Aniello Sgaraglia for the exotic narrative of the alcove, ordering several reworkings in the neoclassical fashion of the day. Thus, faded the glory of the old baroque movement, its taste for hyperbole and sensual variation made way for a new, limpid, modern artistic sensibility.

PALAZZO BISCARI
CATANIA, SICILY

Catania suffered more than any other Sicilian city in the 1693 earthquake. Little survived the awful violence of the tremor and the city had to be rebuilt from scratch amid widespread destruction and huge piles of rubble. The planners of modern Catania took advantage of the disaster to add to the original town plan two main thoroughfares intersecting at right angles in Piazza del Duomo. These neatly divide the city into four districts. The herculean rebuilding effort began swiftly after the catastrophe, under the supervision of the local bishop and the only architect left alive and active, Alonzo di Benedetto. In 1695, two years after the devastation of the earthquake, a *palazzo* owned by the Paternò Castello family, princes of Biscari, was demolished because of the serious structural damage occasioned by the tremor. It stood roughly where the modern building is, but was lower than the city walls. The viceroy decided to rebuild Catania incorporating the old city walls, part of which had survived. His name was de Uzeda, the same name that the nineteenth-century verismo writer Federico de Roberto would later give to the avaricious noble family in his most famous novel, *I Vicerè* (The Viceroys), a richly colored, uncompromising portrait of Sicily in the traumatic period of transition from Bourbon rule to the new monarchs from Piedmont, the Savoys. Only a small number of noble families enjoyed the privilege of building their residences higher than the level of the walls. One such was the princely house of Biscari, which was to construct Catania's most remarkable *palazzo*.

From 1702, there were many architectural interventions on the new

edifice at the initiative of the seventeen-year-old Vincenzo, who had recently become the fourth prince of Biscari. It was Vincenzo who, one year later, "with the most superb magnificence had already commenced to rebuild his estate of houses. . . and to the greater decoration and ornament of this city had purchased divers houses. . . ." Very young, but endowed with extremely clear ideas, the nobleman from Catania set out confidently to implement an ambitious program of construction. A factor agreement dated 1707 mentions the name of Antonino Amato from Messina, engaged for "seven large carved windows in white stone . . .. for the prospect facing the harbor," on two adjacent sides and of two apertures with different designs in the great court. The entrances on the seaward-facing facade are embellished with a riotous array of *putti*, garlands, and scrolls in relief, marked off by richly

carved pillars. Two old men support ornamental *fascias*, themselves bearing a telamon shouldering a capital. The seaward-facing frontage is lent movement by large windows and the regularly spaced pillars in an exaggeratedly baroque *horror vacui* effect. Its spaces teem with a dizzying abundance of decorative vitality that combines learned stylistic references with an enthusiastically vernacular verve.

One is reminded of similar contemporary examples, such as the splendid churches at Lecce, and even certain extreme creations of Spanish baroque in the American colonies. Other

documents, dating from the first decade of the eighteenth century, reveal the likely involvement as designer and site manager of Alonzo di Benedetto from Catania. Regarding the interior, we know that the stucco and gilt decoration of the "four great rooms of the house," the reception areas corresponding to the main entrances of the same facade, had been completed before 1731. However, a new, fervid season of change was looming. In 1739, further renovation was carried out, prompted by the imminent wedding of Vincenzo Paternò's eldest child and heir, Ignazio and perhaps even more by the arrival of new decorative and architectural

fashions from the more up-to-date cities on the mainland. The evangelizer of these new doctrines was Giovan Battista Vaccarini, who had absorbed them in Rome, where had resided in the early 1720s. Palermo-born Vaccarini appointed, in 1730, "prefect commissioner architect of works in the city" by the Senate. He transformed the face of Catania's built heritage with his huge creative influence, which combined the styles of Bernini and Borromini through the filters of Carlo Fontana and his contemporaries, Alessandro Specchi and Francesco de Sanctis. Nor should we forget that the greatest architect of this generation, Filippo Juvarra, was Sicilian and had been able to study thanks to the patronage of the same Cardinal Ottoboni who had summoned Vaccarini from Palermo. Returning to Palazzo Biscari, we find another, more modern intervention, to plans by the engineer, Giuseppe Palazzotto, implemented between 1743 and 1764. During these operations, the external facades, and those facing onto the courtyard, were altered and completed. Some interiors were redecorated and it was also decided to erect a new wing on the east side of the building to house the apartments of the newlyweds. After Vincenzo died in 1744, it was not long before the intellectual stature of his successor became apparent. Ignazio had established a network of important acquaintances during his frequent travels in Europe and was also a keen connoisseur of music and theater, a collector of art and archeological antiquities, and a patron of archeological excavations in and around Catania. The first dig at Herculaneum by Baron d'Hancarville, which excited vast international interest, was carried out in 1747. Giuseppe Palazzotto died in 1764 and his place was taken by Francesco Battaglia, to whom we owe the new building, finished in 1766, to the south east of the original complex. As Anthony Blunt wrote in his fascinating *Sicilian Baroque*, Battaglia's work here is a unique instance in the history of architecture in the city, because it combines elements from the contemporary local style with a fantastic vein that had not yet reached Catania. In this regard, Blunt points out the roofs of the pavilions on the terrace, whose curving lines are reminiscent of the taste for chinoiseries, or the *salone*, which Battaglia transformed in to the center of the *palazzo*. Battaglia and Prince Ignazio, himself an amateur architect, made up a well-matched team to which we owe the

Facing:
The *Galleria degli Uccelli*, or Bird Gallery, has a Neapolitan majolica floor and console tables surmounted by large mirrors set in elaborate gilt frames. The tables are made in such a way as to form small shelves for displaying oriental porcelain.

Left:
A yellow owl painted on a wood panel under one of the console tables in the *Galleria degli Uccelli*. The gallery owes its name to the ornithological theme of its decoration, which continues into the subsequent rooms, and pays tribute to the eclectic learning of Ignazio Paternò Castello, prince of Biscari.

Below right:
The airy stucco staircase leading to the orchestra gallery was designed by the architect Francesco Battaglia in collaboration with skilled master stuccoists. It lies at the end of a narrow corridor that was probably frescoed by Sebastiano Lo Monaco.

new, classicizing mien of the exterior, and the elegant lines of some of the private rooms in the apartment to the south. The extension to the seaward-facing frontage was added in 1764 and 1765, in correspondence to the gallery adjoining the ballroom. Here, too, we may observe a classically informed style. Three high round-arch windows are flanked by pairs of columns and pilaster strips, surmounted by an entablature on capitals.

The following year, some of the private rooms in the new building were decorated superbly in the rocaille idiom. Among them were the *Galleria degli Uccelli* (Bird Gallery) and the *Stanza di Don Chisciotte* (Don Quixote Room), two of the finest examples of chinoiserie in the whole of Sicily. The sparklingly sophisticated decoration of the *Galleria degli Uccelli* continues up to the ivory ceiling, which is traced with sparser gilt stucco floral designs and medallions on a pale green background, portraying alternate figures in Chinese dress and Asian scenes. It is a perfect example of the light, gentle refinement of rococo. Bizarre consoles on the walls are surmounted by large, gilt mirrors and interspersed with narrower ones. Around the frames of the former, and in the latter, sinuously emerging straight from the plate, numerous gracefully intertwining shelves stand ready to display the "Japanese porcelain," the "Porcelain statues from the Indies, from China, [and]

from the factory in Paris, the latest fashion," purchased in Naples in 1766 with the majolica tiles for the floor. The pyrotechnic, sumptuously ornamental effect is very similar to that produced by the two valuable chinoiserie *poudreuses* hidden behind the back wall of the *Galleria degli Specchi* at Palazzo Gangi in Palermo.

Here, the register is more restrained. It is fresher, livelier, more absolutely, precisely rocaille than the glittering gold in the contemporary interiors of Palazzo Gangi. The present furnishings of the gallery are still the eighteenth-century ones that were made specifically for this unique space. However, the doors, panels, and paneling squares with their painting of all kinds of native and exotic birds in natural poses are what gives the name to this cozy gallery with its air of intimate elegance. The *Stanza di Don Chisciotte*, or conversation room, continued the ornithological theme suggested by Prince Ignazio's eclectic learning. In this case, it provides a *basso continuo* in counterpoint to the series of paintings depicting *Episodes from Don Quixote de la Mancha*, doubtfully attributed to the brush of Sebastiano Lo Monaco. The iconographic source for these paintings must have been the famous series of cartoons for tapestries completed by Charles Antoine Coypel for the Gobelins royal tapestry manufactory under Louis XV. They were enormously popular all over Europe, thanks to the cycle of engravings that illustrated Cervantes' text in an edition published in 1744. A copy of this work is recorded in the inheritance inventories of Palazzo Biscari from the late eighteenth century. A group of Gobelins tapestries from the Don Quixote series can also be found at Capodimonte in Naples. From

1769 until the end of the 1780s, a steady procession of artists and craft workers arrived at Palazzo Biscari to embellish the interiors. One name that recurs is Antonio Emmanuele, known as *Pepe*, who constructed furniture and decorative items.

The splendid, lavishly scenographic decoration of the ballroom was probably finished in time for the wedding of the prince's son, Vincenzo, in 1772. An admiring Anthony Blunt describes this glorious interior, pointing it out as the freest interpretation of rococo decoration to be found in Sicily. The sparkling energy of the rocaille stuccoes is truly magnificent, but above all it is the staircase that astounds. It leads to the orchestra gallery, strategically placed in a cupola over the ceiling of the *salone* and communicating with it by means of a skylight. The staircase rises in a spiral, its wave-like progression edged with a spray of volutes in a soft cloud of Tiepolesque whimsy. Probably a product of the

Facing:
The ballroom was probably finished in 1772. The Rococo-inspired decoration is executed in a technique that recalls examples from Bavaria, such as the Nymphenburg Kaisersaal, or the superb stuccoes in some of Venice's noble residences.

collaboration of Battaglia and skilled master stuccoers, the staircase stands at the end of the narrow gallery whose vault may well have been painted by Sebastiano Lo Monaco. This is a masterpiece of skill and agility. It recalls similar illusionistic works in central Europe and the heritage of the Ticino masters, Abbondio Stazio and Carpoforo Mazzetti, whose stucco embellishments transfigured so many Venetian interiors during the eighteenth century. True, it is odd that a disciple of the classical ideals rediscovered in those years of neoclassicism, as was Ignazio Paternò, should be the patron for such an exquisite rocaille decorative scheme. In the early 1780s, Matteo Desiderato and his probable pupil Sebastiano Lo Monaco, were summoned to fresco several rooms in the *palazzo*.

Desiderato is usually attributed with the allegorical works in the smaller panels of the ballroom ceiling whereas critics generally prefer to ascribe to Lo Monaco the *Glory of the Biscari Family*, painted on the dome that rises over the perforation in the middle of the vault. The stuccoes are thought to have been completed by Gioacchino Gianforma and Ignazio Maffeo, who worked with Lo Monaco on several projects in eastern Sicily. In the early decades of the eighteenth century, Sicily could also boast one of the finest exponents of stucco ever in the peerless Giacomo Serpotta. The sources of inspiration, here as for the Lugano masters active in Venice, may have been the rocaille and baroque repertoires of the French textile manufactories of Beauvais and Gobelins, which had been popularized by widely circulated engravings. Again in the 1780s, the garden of the west court was renovated with four small pagoda-roof pavilions at the rear. Fichera claims they were put up by Stefano Ittar, an architect of Tuscan origin who had trained at Rome, where he absorbed the classicizing manner fashionable in cardinal Albani's circle in the middle of the century. From 1765, Ittar was in Catania and the prince of Biscari persuaded him to remain. Ittar was the most interesting architect of the subsequent generation at Catania. He married the daughter of Francesco Battaglia, thus binding himself even more closely to the milieu at the Biscari residence. Battaglia continued his program, building the Biscari theater and concentrating on the new museum. The nucleus of the "museum building adjacent to our house" had already been started between 1752 and 1757 to plans by Palazzotto and it gradually grew up in the series of rooms arranged around two new courtyards to house the many collections of antiquities, paintings, and natural history exhibits that the enlightened nobleman was continually expanding. Grand tourists, distinguished guests, and the merely curious flocked to Biscari to visit the museum, attracted by Prince Ignazio's growing fame as a collector and man of culture. On 3 May 1787, Johann Wolfgang von Goethe was received at the *palazzo*. In his diary, he noted, "I learned something else, allowing myself to be led, with some advantage, by Winkelmann's unbroken thread guiding us through the various periods of art." There is not a single word, obviously, on the architecture and décor of the building, which must have appeared ugly and obsolete to an exponent of the radical neoclassical avant-garde like the great German writer.

Comte De Borch seems to have been a little more interested. *In his Lettres sur la Sicile et sur l'Ile de Malthe* (Letters on Sicily and the Island of Malta), written in 1777 and published in 1782, De Borch says of Palazzo Biscari, "*Si son exterieur n'affiche pas beaucop de magnificence, l'interieur compense bien ce défaut par les beautés qu'il renferme*" (Although the exterior does not flaunt much pomp, the interior makes up for this with the beauty it contains). The great season of construction at the *palazzo* came to an end with the death of Francesco Battaglia. In 1788, he was replaced by his son Antonino, who partially reconfigured the main courtyard and incorporated an adjacent edifice, comprising a number of housing units that formerly belonged to Baron Raddusa, ending with the stables and the main gateway that opens onto the *piazza*. Palazzo Biscari, a splendid example of the aristocratic love of art and tradition, is today almost intact and perfectly conserved, a rare circumstance, particularly in Sicily, where earthquakes, neglect, speculation, and the devastation of war have severely depleted the heritage of noble buildings. Now owned by the noble Moncada Paternò family, Palazzo Biscari delightfully illustrates the taste of the eighteenth century and the striking intellectual journey of the man who once lived there.

BIBLIOGRAPHY

AA.VV., *Gli ultimi Medici. Il tardo barocco a Firenze, 1670–1743*, exhibition catalog edited by M. Chiarini and F.J. Cummings, Florence 1974. AA.VV., *Lo Studiolo d'Isabelle d'Este*, a cura di Silvye Béguin, Paris 1975. AA.VV., *Gli Uffizi. Catalogo generale*, Florence 1979. AA.VV., *Firenze e la Toscana dei Medici nell'Europa del Cinquecento*, exhibition catalog, Florence 1980. AA.VV., *Palazzo Mattei di Giove: le fasi della costruzione e l'individuazione delle lavorazioni caratteristiche*, in "Ricerche di storia dell'arte," n. 20, Rome 1983. AA.VV., *"La bellissima maniera." Alessandro Vittoria e la scultura veneta del Cinquecento*, catalog by Andrea Bacchi, Lia Camerlengo, Manfred Leithe-Jasper, Trento 2000. AA.VV. (edited by Raffaella Morselli), *Gonzaga. La Celeste Galeria*, exhibition catalog, vol. 2, Milan 2002. AA.VV., *I dipinti di Venezia*, Udine 2002. AA.VV., *Il Neoclassicismo in Italia, da Tiepolo a Canova*, exhibition catalog, Milan 2002. Acidini Luchinat, C. (edited by) *Tesori dalle Collezioni Medicee*, Florence 1997. Acidini Luchinat, *Magnificenza alla corte dei Medici. Arte a Firenze alla fine del Cinquecento*, exhibition catalog edited by C.Gregori, M.Heikamp, D.Paolucci, A., Milan 1997. Ackerman, J.S., *Palladio*, Turin 1972. Ackerman, J.S., *La Villa*, Turin 1992. Acton, H., *The last Medici*, London 1958. Acton, H., *Ville Toscane*, Florence 1973. Acton, H., *I Borboni di Napoli*, (1734–1825), Florence 1985, 1997. Alberti, L.B., *L'Architettura (De re aedificatoria)* edited by G. Orlandi and P. Portoghesi, vol. 2, Milan, 1966. Anceschi, L., *Del Barocco e altre prove*, Florence 1953. Angelini, A., *Gian Lorenzo Bernini e i Chigi, tra Roma e Siena*, Milan 1998. Argan, G.C., *The Renaissance City*, London 1969. Assunto, R., *Ambivalenza dell'estetica settecentesca: classicismo e barocco*, relazione al Convegno sulla *Disputa fra classicismo e barocco*, Accademia delle Scienze, Turin 1970. Assunto, R., *Il paesaggio e l'estetica*, Naples 1973. Assunto, R., *Filosofia del giardino e filosofia nel giardino*, Rome 1981. Azzi Visentini, M. (edited by), *Il giardino veneto*, Milan 1988. Bagatti Valsecchi, P.F., *Tipologia della Villa italiana*, in *Ville d'Italia*, Milan 1972. Baltrusaitis, J., *Aberrations*, Paris 1957. Balzaretti, L., *Ville venete*, Milan 1965. Banti, A., *Europa Milleseicentosei, diario di viaggio di Bernardo Bizoni*, Milan 1942. Barbieri, G., *Andrea Palladio e la cultura veneta del Rinascimento*, Rome 1983. Bargellini, P., *I Medici. Storia di una grande famiglia*, Florence 1980. Barocchi, P. (edited by), *Trattati d'arte del Cinquecento*, Bari 1960. Barocchi, P. (edited by), *Palazzo Vecchio: committenza e collezionismo medicei, 1537–1610*, exhibition catalog, Florence 1980. Belli Barsali, I.Puppi, L.Sciolla, G.C., *Le Grandi Ville Italiane*, Veneto, Toscana, Lazio, Novara 1983–1998. Bellonci, M., *Segreti dei Gonzaga*, Milan 1947. Bellonci, M., *Tu, vipera gentile*, Milan 1972. Bellonci, M., *Rinascimento privato*, Milan 1985. Beltrami, D., *La penetrazione economica dei Veneziani in terraferma: forze lavoro e proprietà fondiaria nelle campagne venete dei secoli XVII e XVIII*, Venice 1961. Berti, L., *Il principe dello Studiolo. Francesco I dei Medici e la fine del Rinascimento fiorentino*, Florence 1962. Blunt, A., *Sicilian Baroque*, London 1968. Blunt, A., *Neapolitan Baroque and Rococo Architecture*, London 1975. Bonelli Conenna, L.Pacini, E. (edited by), *Vita in villa nel Senese, dimore, giardini e fattorie*, Pisa 2000. Borch, M.J. de, *Lettres sur la Sicile e sur l'ile de Malthe. de Monsieur de Borch . . .*, Turin 1782. Borsi, F., *L'architettura del principe*, Florence 1980. Boscarino, S., *Sicilia barocca*, Rome 1986. Brandi, C., *Disegno della Pittura Italiana*, Turin 1980. Braudel, F., *Civiltà e Imperi del Mediterraneo nell'Età di Filippo II*, Turin, 1955. Braudel, F., *Civilisation matérielle, économie et capitalisme (XV–XVIII siècle), les jeux de l'échange*, Paris 1979. Briganti, G., *La Maniera italiana*, Rome 1961. Brignone Cattaneo, E.Schezen, R., *Le grandi dimore genovesi*, Turin 1992. Brosses de, C., *Voyage d'Italie*, Paris, 1739; 1846–47. Callari, L., *I Palazzi di Roma*, third edition, Rome 1944. Camporesi, P., *Le belle contrade (nascita del paesaggio italiano)*, Milan 1992. Caneva, C. (edited by), *Power and Glory. Medici Portraits from the Uffizi Gallery*, exhibition catalog, The Pennsylvania Academy of Fine Arts, Philadelphia 2001. Caneva, C.Lincoln, E.Wzerner, C. (edited by), *Crafting the Medici. Patrons and Artisans in Florence, 1537–1737*, exhibition catalog, David Winton Bell Gallery, Brown University, Providence 1999. Canova, A. (edited by), *Di villa in villa. Guida alla visita delle Ville Venete*, Treviso 1990. Cevese, R., *Ville della provincia di Vicenza*, Milan 1971. Chastel, A., *Art et humanisme à Florence au temps de Laurent le Magnifique*, Paris 1959. Chiarini, M. (edited by), *Visite reali a Palazzo Pitti. Ritratti dal XVI al XVIII secolo*, exhibition catalog, Florence 1995. Chiarini de, A.G., *Leopoldo de' Medici e la sua raccolta di disegni nel "Carteggio d'Artisti" dell'Archivio di Stato di Firenze*, in "Paragone." 1975. Chierici, G., *Il palazzo italiano dal secolo XVI al secolo XIX*, Milan 1964. Clark, K., *Il paesaggio nell'arte*, Milan 1985. Coffin, M., *The Villa in the Life of Renaissance*, Rome, Princeton 1979. Colasanti, A., *Case e palazzi barocchi di Roma*, Milan 1912. Combescot, P., *Les petites Mazarines*, Paris 1999. Coniglio, G. (edited by), *Mantova. La storia*, I, Mantova 1991. Cosgrove, D., *Il paesaggio palladiano* (edited by Francesco Vallerani), Centro Internazionale di Studi di Architettura "Andrea Palladio," Vicenza 2000. Cosgrove, D., *Social Formation and Symbolic Landscape*, London, 1984. Costant, C., *The Palladio Guide*, London 1985. Cresti, C.Listri, M., *Civiltà delle Ville toscane*, Udine 1992. Cresti, C.Rendina, C.Listri, M., *Ville e Palazzi di Roma*, Udine 1998. Crosato, L., *Gli affreschi nelle ville venete del Cinquecento*, Treviso 1962. Cunaccia, C.Listri, M., *Giardini e Parchi Italiani*, Milan 1995. Cunaccia, C.Listri, M., *Toscana insolita fantastica*, Milan 2000. Cunaccia, C.Listri, M., Signorini, R., *Rivedere Mantova-Storia, cultura e arte di una capitale europea*, Florence 1996. Cunaccia, C.M.-Smith, M.E., *Interni a Venezia*, Venice 1994. Della Pergola, P., *Villa Borghese*, Rome 1962. De Seta, C., *Sulla presunta città barocca*, London 1973. De Seta, C., *Disegni di Luigi Vanvitelli architetto e scenografo*, in AA.VV., *Luigi Vanvitelli*, Napoli 1973. De Seta, C., *Architettura, ambiente e società a Napoli nel 700*, Turin 1981. De Simone, M., *Ville Palermitane del XVII e XVIII secolo*, Genoa 1968 De Simone, M., *Ville Palermitane dal XVI al XVIII secolo*, Palermo 1974. Elias, N., *La civiltà delle buone maniere*, Bologna 1988. Fagiolo dell'Arco, M., *L'immagine al potere. Vita di Giovan Lorenzo Bernini*, Bari 2001. Fagiolo dell'Arco, M.Carandini, S., *L'effimero barocco. Strutture della festa nella Roma del Seicento*, Rome 1978. Fantoni, M., *La Corte del Granduca. Forma e simboli del potere mediceo fra Cinque e Seicento*, Rome 1994. Fariello, F., *Architettura dei giardini*, Rome 1967. Fernandez, D., *Porporino ou les mysteres de Naples*, Paris 1974. Fernandez, D., *La perle et le croissant, l'Europe baroque de Naples à Saint Petersbourg*, Paris 1995. Franzoi, U.Pignatti, T.Wolters, W. (edited by), *Il Palazzo Ducale di Venezia*, Treviso 1990. Fumaroli, M., *L'Ecole du silence, Le sentiment des images au XVII siècle*, Paris 1994. Gavazza, E., *La grande decorazione a Genova*, Genoa 1974. Gavazza, E., *Lo spazio dipinto. Il grande affresco genovese nel '600*, Genoa 1989. Gavazza, E.-Rotondi Terminiello, G., *Genova nell'Età Barocca*, Genoa 1992. Gemin, M.-Pedrocco, F., *Giambattista Tiepolo: i dipinti. Opera completa*, Venice 1993. Giusti, A. (edited by), *Splendori di Pietre dure. L'Arte di corte nella Firenze dei Granduchi*, Florence 1989. Goethe, J.W., *Viaggio in Italia (1786–1788)*, Milan 1975. Golzio, V., *Palazzi di Roma dalla Rinascita al Neoclassico*, Bologna 1971. Gombrich, E.H., *Norm and Form: Studies in the Art of Renaissance*, London 1966 Gonzalez-Palacios, A., *Il Tempio del Gusto*, Milan 1984, 1986. Gonzalez-Palacios, A. (edited by), *Fasto Romano, dipinti, sculture arredi dai palazzi di Roma*, exhibition catalog, Rome 1991. Gonzalez-Palacios, A. (edited by), *Pietro Piffetti e gli ebanisti a Torino*, Turin 1992. Gonzalez-Palacios, A. (edited by), *Il Gusto dei Principi. Arte di Corte del XVII e XVIII secolo*, Milan 1993. Gonzalez-Palacios, A., *L'Armadio delle Meraviglie*, Milan 1997. Griseri, A., *Le metamorfosi del Barocco*, Turin 1967. Griseri, A., *Ambienti del Settecento*, Novara 1985. Gros, H., *Roma nel Settecento*, Bari 1990. Grosso, O., *Dimore genovesi dal secolo XVI al XIX*, in *Liguria*, Milan 1955. Guerrini, L., *Palazzo Mattei di Giove: le antichità*, Rome 1982. Hamburg, P.-G., *The Villa of Lorenzo il Magnifico at Poggio a Caiano and the origin of Palladianism*, in *Idea and Form: Studies in the History of Art*, 1959. Harris, J., *The Palladians*, London 1981. Haskell, F., *Mecenati e pittori, Studio sui rapporti fra arte e società italiana nell'età barocca*, Florence 1985. Hibbard, H., *The Architecture of the Palazzo Borghese*, Rome 1962. Honour, H., *L'arte della cineseria*, Florence 1963. Houel, J.P.L.L., *Voyage pittoresque des îles de Sicile, de Malte et de Lipari*, Paris 1782–87. Jaffè, M., *Rubens and Italy*, Oxford 1979. Lalande de, J.J.L., *Voyage en Italie, contenant l'histoire et les anedoctes les plus singulières de l'Italie et sa description. . ., Paris 1768. Langedijk, K., *The Portraits of the Medici. XVth.-XVIIIth. Centuries*, Florence 1981, 1983. Lanza Tomasi, G., *Le ville di Palermo*, Palermo 1965. Lauro, G., *Palazzi diversi nell'alma città di Roma*, Rome 1655. Levey, M., *Tiepolo's treatment of classical story at Villa Valmarana*, in "Journal of the Warburg and Courtauld Institutes." 1957. Lévi-Strauss, C., *Regarder, écouter, lire*, Paris 1993. Librando, V., *Palazzo Biscari in Catania*, Catania 1965. Litta, P., *Famiglie celebri italiane*, Milan and Turin 1819–1891. Lugli, A., *Naturalia et Mirabilia. Il collezionismo enciclopedico delle Wunderkammer in Europa*, Milan 1983. Mahon, D., *Studies in Seicento art and Theory*, London 1947. Manilli, J., *Villa Borghese fuori Porta Pinciana*, Rome 1650. Maravall, J.A., *La cultura del Barroco, Analisis de una estructura historica*, Sant Joan Despì (Barcelona) 1975. Marcenaro, G., *Viaggiatori stranieri in Liguria*, Genova 1987. Masson, G., *Giardini d'Italia*, Milan 1961. Mauro, E., *Le ville a Palermo*, Palermo 1992. Mazzotti, G. (edited by), *Le ville venete*, anastatica reprint of the third edition, 1954, preface by L. Puppi, Treviso 1987. Mignani, D., *Le ville medicee di Giusto Utens*, Florence 1982. Montelatici, D., *Villa Borghese fuori Porta Pinciana*, Rome 1700. Muraro, M.Marton, P., *Civiltà delle Ville Venete*, Fagagna, Udine 1986. Neil, E.H., *Architecture in Context: the Villas of Bagheria, Sicily*, PhD Dissertation, Harvard University, 1995. Palladio, A., *I quattro libri dell'architettura di Andrea Palladio*, Dominico and de' Franceschi, Venetia 1570, anastatica reprint, Milan 1980. Pallucchini, R., *Gli affreschi nelle Ville Venete dal Seicento all'Ottocento*, vol. 2, Venice 1978. Pane, R., *Bernini architetto*, Venice 1953. Panofsky, E., *Studi di iconologia. I temi umanistici nell'arte del rinascimento*, Turin 1975. Pertica, D., *Villa Borghese*, Rome 1990. Pevsner, N., *Storia dell'architettura europea*, Bari 1966. Pieraccini, G., *La stirpe dei Medici di Cafaggiolo*, Florence 1924 Poleggi, E., *Strada Nuova. Una lottizzazione del Cinquecento a Genova*, Genoa 1968. Poliziano, A., *Le selve e la strega: prolusioni nello studio fiorentino (1482–1492)*, edited by I. del Lungo, Florence 1925. Pomian, K., *Collezionisti, amatori e curiosi, Parigi-Venezia XVI–XVIII secolo*, Turin 1987. Portoghesi, P., *Roma barocca*, Rome 1968. Portoghesi, P., *Architettura del Rinascimento a Roma*, Milan 1979. Praz, M., *Bellezza e bizzarria*, Milan 1960. Praz, M., *La filosofia dell'arredamento*, Milan 1964. Praz, M., *Gusto Neoclassico*, Milan 1974. Praz, M., *Il mondo che ho visto*, Milan 1982. Puppi, L., *I Tiepolo a Vicenza e le statue dei "nani" di Villa Valmarana a S. Bastiano*, in "Atti dell'Istituto Veneto di Scienze, Lettere ed Arti," 1967–68. Puppi, L., *Andrea Palladio: opera completa*, Milan, 1973. Puppi, L. (edited by), *Alvise Cornaro e il suo tempo*, catalog, Padua 1980. Puppi, L., *Andrea Palladio: il testo, l'immagine, la città. Bibliografia e iconografia palladiane; cartografia vicentina; Palladio accademico olimpico*, Milan 1980. Robb, P., *M. L'enigma Caravaggio*, Milan 2001. Rubens, P.P., *I Palazzi moderni di Genova raccolti e disegnati da Pietro Paolo Rubens*, Anvers 1622. Saint Non, J.C.R. de, *Voyage pitoresque, ou Description des Royames de Naples et de Sicile*, Paris 1781–1786. Saramago, J., *Andrea Mantegna. Un'etica, un'estetica*, a cura di Luciana Stegagno Picchio, Genoa 2002. Sciascia, L.La Duca, R., *Palermo Felicissima*, Palermo 1973. Siracusano, C., *La pittura del Settecento in Sicilia*, Rome 1986. Spinosa, A., *Gli anni di Carlo e Ferdinando di Borbone (1734–1805): continuità e crisi di una tradizione*, in AA.VV., *Civiltà del '700 a Napoli 1734–1799*, exhibition catalog, Florence 1979. Strazzullo, F., *Le lettere di Luigi Vanvitelli nella Biblioteca palatina di Caserta*, Galatina 1976. Suida, W., *Genua*, Leipzig 1906. Tafuri, M., *Committenze e tipologia nelle ville palladiane*, in "Bollettino del Centro Internazionale di Studi di Architettura Andrea Palladio," XI, Vicenza 1969. Tafuri, M., *Jacopo Sansovino e l'architettura del '500 a Venezia*, Padua 1969. Tafuri, M., *Venezia e il Rinascimento*, Turin 1982 Tagliolini, A., *I giardini di Roma*, Rome 1980. Tedesco, N., *Villa Palagonia*, Palermo 1988. Torselli, G., *I palazzi di Roma*, Milan 1965. Trevelyan, R., *Principi sotto il vulcano*, Berkeley 1982. Valtieri, S., *Il palazzo del principe, il palazzo del cardinale, il palazzo del mercante nel Rinascimento*, Rome 1988. Vasari, G., *Vite de' più eccellenti architetti, pittori e scultori italiani. . .*, vol. II, edited by G. Milanesi, Florence 1906. Viale, V., *Mostra del Barocco Piemontese*, exhibition catalog, Turin 1963. Wharton, E., *Ville Italiane e loro giardini*, Florence 1998. Wind, E., *Misteri pagani nel Rinascimento*, Milan 1971. Wittkower, R., *Palladio e il Palladianesimo*, Turin 1984. Wolters, W., *Storia e politica nei dipinti di Palazzo Ducale. Aspetti dell'autocelebrazione della Repubblica di Venezia nel Cinquecento*, Venezia 1987. Wolters, W., *Architettura e decorazione nel Cinquecento veneto*, in "Annali di Architettura," n. 4–5, 1992–93. Yates, F., *L'arte della memoria*, Turin 1972. Zaccagnini, G., *Le ville di Roma*, Rome 1976. Zalapì, A., *Dimore di Sicilia*, Venezia 1998. Zeri, F., *Pittura e Controriforma*, Turin 1957. Ziino, V., *Contributi allo studio dell'Architettura del '700 in Sicilia*, Palermo 1950. Zorzi, A.Marton, P., *I Palazzi Veneziani*, Fagagna (Udine) 1989. Zorzi, G., *Le ville e i teatri di Andrea Palladio*, Venezia 1969.

ACKNOWLEDGMENTS

Sincere thanks are due to the owners of the private residences
for their kind permission to take photographs.
In particular, the author wishes to thank the princes Borromeo Arese, Signor Andrea Boscu,
the Marquises Cattaneo Adorno, Father Prospero Colonna, Countess Giovanna Giustiniani Moncada, Lord Lambton,
Countess Anna Provana di Collegno, Count Lodovico di Valmarana,
Countess Cecilia di Valmarana for Villa Valmarana ai Nani, and the Versace family.
The author would also like to express his gratitude to Professor Nicola Spinosa, superintendent of the artistic
and historical heritage for Naples and province, Professor Claudio Strinati, special superintendent for museums in Rome,
and Professor Domenico Valentino, superintendent of the environmental
and architectural heritage of Florence, Prato, and Pistoia.
Thanks also go to Dona Sandra Cattan Naslausky, former ambassador of Brazil to the Holy See,
and to the architect Toni Facella Sensi, for their kind cooperation.
Cesare Cunaccia particularly wishes to thank Elisabetta Feruglio of Magnus Edizioni for her unfailing, stimulating,
and wise reflections during the drafting of the texts, and Federica Cappabianca
for her invaluable, patient technical support and consistently valid assistance along the byways of the book's research.
For Massimo Listri, a joy and torment in every sense, mere words are not enough. He will understand.
Finally, a warm and very special "thank you" to Cesare Lucioli who, as ever, has generously provided support
and protection, above all from myself, during the birth and maturation of this volume.

PHOTOGRAPHY CREDITS

ALL THE PHOTOGRAPHS IN THIS BOOK ARE BY MASSIMO LISTRI WITH THE EXCEPTION OF THE FOLLOWING:

GIORGIO GNEMMI: P. 42, P. 43, PP. 44-45, P. 46, P. 50
FRANCESCA DE COL TANA: P. 47
DARIO TACCHINI: PP. 48-49
ARCHIVIO AMMINISTRAZIONE ISOLE BORROMEO: P. 51
ARCHIVIO ALINARI: P. 60, P. 61 BOTTOM, P. 62 BOTTOM
PIERO ORLANDI: PP. 60-61, P. 61 TOP, P. 62 TOP, P. 63
EBS-ARSENALE EDITRICE (GIORGIO RUZZENE): P. 64, PP. 64-65
ARCHIVIO FOTOGRAFICO QUATTRONE: PP. 74-75, P. 147
ARCHIVIO MAGNUS: PP. 4-5, PP. 10-11, DA P. 78 A P. 137 (PAOLO MARTON), P. 144,
P. 146, P. 169 BOTTOM (PAOLO MARTON), P. 171 (PAOLO MARTON), PP. 178-179 (PAOLO MARTON),
P. 187 TOP (PAOLO MARTON)